HAPPY PLANTS, HAPPY YOU

Quarto.com

© 2023 Quarto Publishing Group USA Inc.
Text © 2023 Kamili Bell Hill
Illustration © 2023 Paula Champagne

First Published in 2023 by Cool Springs Press, an imprint of The Quarto Group,
100 Cummings Center, Suite 265-D, Beverly, MA 01915, USA.
T (978) 282-9590 F (978) 283-2742

Cool Springs Press titles are also available at discount for retail, wholesale, promotional, and bulk purchase. For details, contact the Special Sales Manager by email at specialsales@quarto.com or by mail at The Quarto Group, Attn: Special Sales Manager, 100 Cummings Center, Suite 265-D, Beverly, MA 01915, USA.

27 26 25 24 23   1 2 3 4 5

ISBN: 978-0-7603-7950-9

Digital edition published in 2023
eISBN: 978-0-7603-7951-6

Library of Congress Cataloging-in-Publication Data is available.

Design: Cindy Samargia Laun
Photography: Christina Bohn Photography; except Kamili Bell Hill on pages 7 and 170, Eddie Hill on page 12, Taji Riley on page 166, and Shutterstock on pages 4–5, 25, 66, 82, 89, 96, 112, 124, 141, 148, and 153
Illustrations: Paula Champagne

Printed in China

HAPPY PLANTS, HAPPY YOU

A Plant-Care & Self-Care Guide for the Modern Houseplant Parent

KAMILI BELL HILL
creator of @plantblerd

COOL
SPRINGS
PRESS

"Okay, talk about a game-changer! Plant mom-ing should feel refreshing, not daunting. From finally figuring out what I've been doing wrong to learning alternative ways to pamper my plant babies beyond watering them, this book is filled with the kind of *a-ha!* moments that give me the clarity and confidence to find my way to plant parent peace."

—Ashley Renne Nsonwu of @heyashleyrenne and author of
The Vegan Baby Cookbook and Guide

"*Happy Plants, Happy You* is the much-needed fresh take on the world of plants and gardening. Combining interior design, self-care, and plant-care tips that you can trust, Kamili brings her unique sense of humor, style, and design sensibility to this fun and informative book. Kamili's extensive experience and endearing personality will have readers walking away both more confident in their own plant parenthood journey and feeling like they've made a new friend. This is a must-add to any plant lover's collection."

—Gloria Alamrew, culture writer and critic

"*Happy Plants, Happy You* is a beautiful balance of visuals and helpful text detailing a unique perspective from a plant lover. As a plant enthusiast myself, this is such a wonderful visual treat, and I enjoyed every page."

—Cyril of Cyril's Urban Jungle, @cyrilcybernated

"A joy to read! Combining plant care with self-care, this beautiful book is full of practical tips—for both you and your plants."

—Roos of @plantwithroos

"Kamili rediscovers the many adventures of indoor jungle lushness, intro-duces the restorative rejuvenation of bringing nature into our homes, dives into the plethora of life lessons our plants can offer us, and guides readers on a viridescent journey so that they, too, can reconnect with nature. From one Black plant nerd to another, Kamili, thank you for sharing your magic and your story with us so generously."

—@plantkween

"Kamili is a dope spirit whom I've had the actual pleasure of meeting in real life. The energy she exudes in person is demonstrated in this book. It is knowledgeable, helpful, and overall a good read to assist you on your plant journey."

—Kevin, digital creator, @theplantpapi

"Kamili calls out our challenging relationship with hustle culture and invites us to learn to love on ourselves by utilizing the healing of house-plants. She then wraps her arms around us with a beginner-friendly guide to helping your plants flourish. I can say *Happy Plants, Happy You* is named properly!"

—Dominique Edouard of @domslittlegarden

"Prepare to feel inspired after reading Kamili's all-too-relatable book illus-trating how the plant hobby offers a respite from the burnout of hustle culture. This book is perfect for those looking to take their plant care more seriously and take their lives more lightheartedly."

—Lindsay of alltheplantbabies.com

"I can't 'leaf' this book alone! *Happy Plants, Happy You* has the perfect combination of plant care, anecdotal wit, and New Yorker realness from the most zealous plant fiend I know. Kamili hilariously combines life and plant advice in the style that her social media following has come to love her for. I LOL'ed for real and added some new tips to my plant- AND self-care routine."

—Colah B. Tawkin, host of the *Black in the Garden* podcast

"*Happy Plants, Happy You* does a great job illustrating the life of a plant parent. Kamili really brings readers in by sharing personal accounts around her successes and failures with plants. A nice bonus was how the book brilliantly demonstrates leading a life of intentionality and pursuing things that make you passionate with statements like, 'Why do we stop daydreaming at a certain age?' There is also a wealth of accessible plant-care tips and tricks featured so that plant people of all experience levels have practical knowledge to take with them as they continue their plant parenthood journey."

—Tyler of @thatplantguy_ty

For Eddie, Skye, and Lyric.

"You can do some rather extraordinary things
if that's what you really believe."
—*Toni Morrison*

Contents

The plant parent in her natural habitat. I feel immediately relaxed whenever I am in plant-filled spaces and completely surrounded. My local nursery is one of my favorite places to pop in to get my double dose of greenery.

INTRODUCTION: **How Plants Bring You Peace**

MY JOURNEY TO PLANT MAMAHOOD—THE PATH TO PEACE

Congratulations on taking your first step on the path to peace. I'm guessing you live a busy life, like the rest of us. How can you find time for yourself? I'll show you how—through houseplants! Houseplants are much more than a hobby or a living decorative accent for your home. Houseplants helped me exit the highway to burnout, and they can do the same for you.

We can learn so much about the relationships we have with ourselves and others through our plants if we are just still and listen. You're probably asking, what does she mean by a relationship with yourself? We do have a relationship with ourselves. And like any other relationship, sometimes we need to take a moment to examine it. Is the relationship healthy? Are you giving yourself the same care and attention you give to others with whom you are in a relationship—whether romantic or platonic? Are you giving yourself the same attention, kindness, and, above all, grace? Or are you taking yourself and your needs for granted? Are you putting relationships on the back burner and promising to get to them later—and then later never arrives? The relationship we have with ourselves is easily the most neglected. I was very guilty of neglecting this relationship. Heck, it wasn't until I started caring for plants that I even started thinking of caring for myself as a relationship with me. But, when you think of it in those terms, the basics you are not giving to yourself that you so freely and willingly give to others come into very sharp focus: quality time, attention, kindness, grace, and forgiveness. This is arguably the most important relationship you will ever have. When you treat yourself well, that wellness spreads into all the other areas of your life.

With a collection of a whole lot of houseplants, I don't know the exact number because I never count (it's a rule), I've learned a thing or two about growing—both houseplants and personally. I will share some easy tips to help you build your confidence in growing plants, and show you how these green beings can help you create and maintain a practice of self-care. As your plants grow, you will too. So, let's get to planting!

As soon as you enter our home you are greeted by our botanical besties waiting to welcome you in. Adding plants made the décor literally come alive, and our space became all the more inviting. A fully furnished room is empty without plants.

My two greatest propagations! Looking back, these matching plant jumpsuits were a glimpse into the future.

How Did I Become
a Plant Parent?

MY ORIGIN STORY

Before I became the blerd (Black + nerd) plant parent you've come to know and love (I hope), I worked in corporate tax law at a public accounting firm. It was soul draining and inhospitable to any creativity, joy, or happiness. With its prison gray walls, drab carpeting, and perpetually flickering florescent lights, work was the kind of place where fun went to die. How did I get there? I ask myself that all the time. The answer is fairly simple and plain: I was a freshly minted law school graduate with a stack of student loan bills staring at me. The offer of gainful employment, when I knew so many who were without it, was just too tempting and hard to resist.

That's something they did not tell us when we signed up. Getting a law degree was not at all like our favorite legal eagle television shows that romanced more than a few of us. There was no fast-paced job in a glamourous glass skyscraper waiting for the new graduates. Well, maybe for a handful. The rest of us would have to scrape and claw and take whatever came our way. So, I did what I had to do. I schlepped to a nondescript job in the gray, windowless building. Needless to say, the decision to take a career break after my first daughter was born was an EASY one. I call it a career break, but it was more like an escape. I was free of those gray walls and endless hours of boring tax research!

But life on the outside wasn't always easy. I had a law degree, and I was a stay-at-home mom. No one was more surprised than me at this turn of events. It was not something that I ever imagined myself capable of doing—make no mistake, it was one of the hardest jobs to take on. There was no time off, and, worse, there are no bosses more demanding than a hangry three-year-old also in desperate need of a nap. It's not the twos that are terrible; it's pretty much the entirety of the toddler years. My daughter, who was absolutely adorable, ruled our house with an iron fist. And her little sister, well, when she came along it was like she had a score to settle. We had zero sleep for the entire first two years of her life. That whole "sleep when they sleep" advice they give new parents is rubbish. There are far too many other things that need to be done while children are sleeping.

So, there I was—staying at home, keeping house, and raising my two girls. While I loved it and am grateful for having had the opportunity to do it, I have to be completely honest: It was both the most rewarding time and the most isolating time.

And then there was the insecurity. Every time someone asked, "What do you do?" I felt judged, when all they had done was ask an innocent question. No matter who asked, the heat always rose up from under my shirt to light my face on fire whenever I was faced with that fairly harmless question. The solution? I busied myself. Like, really, really busied! The fear of judgement from others made me overcompensate and stretch myself really thin. There was no board, or organization, or cause that I did not volunteer for. While I do love volunteering, I did not have to say yes to *everything*. But say yes I did! I said yes to all, just so I could list everything that I was doing or involved in, so that my answer could be anything besides "just a mom." Of course, there is no such thing as "just a mom." There was nothing simple or easy about staying home with my kids, and I wore many, many hats in that role. But it was hard to unlearn that behavior or even to stop bristling at the question, especially when the question wasn't so much, "What do you do?" but more, "When are you going back to work?" I was literally working every day—just not in an office. But I digress.

It's a love connection! The *Ficus lyrata*, commonly known as the fiddle-leaf fig, made me fall in love with houseplants all over again and paved a path to peace.

This Vanilla Strawberry™ shrub is one of the many hydrangeas that I have planted over the years in my yard. They remind me of my maternal grandmother. She filled every corner of her yard with hydrangeas. This Vanilla Strawberry™ started as a 24 inch (61 cm) plant in a gallon-sized pot. It is now over 8 feet (2.4 m) tall and 5 feet (1.5 m) wide!

There is always an upside, at least that is what I believe. In the course of volunteering for every board, organization, and worthy cause, I did a lot of firsts and discovered some new things that I was really great at. Like, great, great. Things I never would have done or had time to do if was working two jobs—the one at the office and then the one at home. The home duties don't go away just because there's an office to go to. I planned many fundraisers, events, and even weddings! In that dabbling, I discovered just how much I loved interior and event design. (It's a wandering path, I know. Just go with it.) As I was doing all of these things that I loved, that did not feel like work, I got an itch (you guessed it) to go back to work outside of the home. But one thing I knew for sure, I could not return to my prior field. I wanted something new, but I really had no idea what. I decided to reinvent myself and try interior design professionally.

It started with a few refresh projects. I'd help my clients update their space with small changes like new lighting fixtures or a new paint color and a few accessories. Small changes that made a big impact and helped them fall in love with their space again. Through design, I re-discovered plants. Whether it was a complete makeover or a design refresh, no job was complete without a houseplant—they literally breathed life into the space. I furnished and decorated an entire apartment in Manhattan that had amazing views of the Empire State Building and was just flooded with natural light in nearly every room. Needless to say, it screamed for plants. But not just any plant, the quintessential designer plant—the fiddle-leaf fig. Believe it or not, prior to using it in that apartment I had only seen it on the pages of my favorite décor magazines and in the background of every show on HGTV. Well, let me tell you—the pictures don't do that plant justice. The leaves are huge and green and glossy! You can probably guess where I'm going with this—yup, I bought one for the client and a small one for myself. It was

the first houseplant that I'd purchased for myself in years.

My mother had an indoor jungle, before it was a trend with that clever nickname. She just had a lot of houseplants. Throughout my childhood, I was always surrounded by plants—both indoors and out. My Saturday list of chores at home included watering or spritzing the plants. One of my very favorite places to hangout to read was in a patch of sunshine next to her giant five-foot (1.5 m) cactus. She had massive Boston ferns and *Ficus benjamina* trees—two of the plants I managed to kill the fastest (more on that later). But this indoor plant love did not carry over into my adulthood. Sure, there was still plant love, but I followed in the footsteps of my maternal grandmother and focused my plant love outside.

My grandmother loved to garden outside. She migrated from Florida to Connecticut. Her way of bringing a little sunshine with her was to fill her yard with fruit trees and flowers. Especially hydrangeas—she planted them everywhere. She had the prettiest yard on her street. I spent many happy afternoons after school running through that yard with my cousins. In turn, when we bought our first home, the first thing I did was fill my yard with the same flowers of my childhood. It was not until I started helping others bring living beauty into their homes that I wanted indoor plants of my own.

Now, some of you may think I'm crazy starting an indoor plant journey with a fiddle-leaf fig—and you might be right. Maybe it's my villain origin story, and I just don't know it yet. But that's what I did. As I cared for this plant with the oversized reputation for drama, it thrived in my care. Watching it push out new leaves week after week was a thrill like no other. To say Fiona—that's what I named her—flipped a switch in me is an understatement. My collection quickly escalated from one plant to many plants. What started as a design tool and hobby I soon learned was SO much more, and I hope the same for you!

When I added plants to this space, it became so much more than a guest room. It's now our room of relaxation, recharging, and unplugging. You won't find any gold mirrors in here.

CHAPTER 1

The To-Do List

How Adding Houseplants to Your To-Do List Translates to Self-Care, Not to More Work

As the CEO and president of my family and household, as well as being a busy volunteer and budding entrepreneur, I was always busy. I wore that busyness on my sleeve. Projecting an air of "get shit done" is both a gift and a curse. Whenever something needed doing, or a seat on some community board needed filling, or an event needed planning, I was on everyone's short list of the first person to ask. I have yet to master the art of saying no (I'm still working on that), so I was busy always. For me, there was only one way to keep track of things—I made lists. Not lists in my head or on the phone. Actual paper lists in a tattered notebook that I did not leave home without.

This fiddle-leaf fig is pushing out new leaves. New leaves on a fiddle-leaf fig emerge from a sheath that covers and protects the tender new-growth bud tissue. When a leaf first emerges, it is tightly wound and slowly opens. It starts out quite small and pale in color. As it continues to grow, it darkens in color and gets bigger. It is quite thrilling to watch the progression!

That saying that the mind remembers what the hand writes is true. It's an old habit that was impossible to break. There was the to-do list for the house, the endless to-do list for the kids, the to-do list for the community projects, the to-do list for the kids' schools, and the to-do list for the boards I sat on. I could go on and on. The list of my lists was endless. But in the writing of these lists, the one person not making it onto a single one of them was me. I was so busy running here and there taking care of everyone and everything, I rarely, if ever, carved out time to do things for myself. Who had time for that? Not me, I had to get all the other stuff done. Now that's not to say I wasn't ever having any fun or enjoyment. Of course I was, but I was not the center of that fun or care. It always involved other people or was in furtherance of some obligation or project. And relaxation? Well, that was just out of the question. The minute I would sit down, my mind would immediately race to something that needed doing.

I was always tired, but what could I do? Some days, my three o'clock afternoon slump started around ten in the morning. But I would just push through it with caffeine—I was totally hopped up on coffee. If I could have rigged up an intravenous drip, I probably would have. I say probably because I'm leaving a little room for logic in this hypothetical scenario, but, really, I know I would have, if I could have accomplished it. Things had to be done, people were relying upon me. I couldn't say no and, especially, could not disappoint anyone after I'd said yes by not getting whatever I had agreed to do done. I was barreling toward a brick wall, but I had not yet figured out how to change course. And to be completely honest, I had not yet figured out that I should change course. I was hustling, and isn't that what we've been told it's all about? Hustle culture had me completely fooled.

Amid the seemingly endless hustle and bustle, I was caring for a houseplant—a fiddle-leaf fig. Well let me back up, I was not really "caring" for it. At least not with any intentionality. I was watering it, and kind of keeping my eye on it as I was coming and going. This is not what I would call a beginner's plant, but it was a super trendy plant. It still is, and probably always will be. It makes quite the statement in any room, with any style of décor. After seeing it on the pages of every single design magazine, I was easily influenced. I guess it wasn't quite peer pressure, since I was the peer applying the pressure to myself. When I bought that one for my client, I just had to have one too.

In the interest of full disclosure: At that time I thought of my fiddle-leaf fig plant as just a design accessory, as living décor. I did exactly what I saw everyone else do, I plunked it down in a corner where she looked fabulous! Initially that is. I absentmindedly took care of it, because I liked the way it looked next to the sofa. It started to droop a bit, so I moved it a little closer to a window in the same room. It still looked pretty posh in its new position—it was all about the aesthetics for me at this point. This beautiful green plant looked great in my family room and added something that had been missing. After the move closer to the light, it stopped drooping and seemed a little happier. Then one day, I leaned in to water it and to my delight I saw that a new leaf had emerged. I was both surprised and excited. The new leaf was tiny and bright green, with a dark papery thing around the edges. I wondered if that new leaf was going to stay tiny and bright green, or would it get bigger and darker like the others? This curiosity made me check that one tiny new leaf just about every day. The days passed, and the leaf did get a little bigger, but no darker. I leaned in for a closer look and there was a weird brown thing that looked like a flower bud peaking up next to the new leaf. I was tempted to peel it open to get a peek inside but decided to leave it alone. And boy was I glad I did—it was another new leaf! Now, before these new leaves started sprouting, I hadn't done one bit of research—as you can tell. I didn't even know that brown bud was the new leaf before the protective sheath dropped off. I knew literally nothing about this plant's needs. In fact, I had not really thought it might have needs beyond just watering it. But there were many more questions to ask: What kind of light does it like? It needs water, but how often? And what about fertilizer? I knew nothing. I was completely winging it, but as the plant began to grow, so did my curiosity. I wanted to know more. Now that it was growing, I wanted to keep that going. I started digging around to find out how I could keep the growth going.

Turns out, I was going about it all wrong! The plant needed way more light than I was providing. Even though I liked how it looked next to the sofa, after what I had read, I knew it would ultimately not survive in that spot. The window where it was sitting was shaded by my covered porch. In fact, with my new plant knowledge, I now realized the room itself was kind of on the dark side. Those three large windows shaded by the porch did not let in much bright light. I needed to put aesthetics aside and give the plant what it needed. I moved it from the family room to a spot right in front of a bright window on the second floor. I had grown attached to this little green plant, and I wanted it to keep growing.

While I had grown up surrounded by plants and remembered helping my mom water all her plants, as an adult, my plant love was relegated to outdoor plants. I think that was due in large part to my past failures. Years ago, when I had an apartment in Harlem, New York, I couldn't wait to fill it with plants.

One of the first plants that I bought was a *Ficus benjamina* tree just like the one of my childhood. I lived in a walk-up apartment, and it was a struggle to get that plant up the stairs. She put up quite a fight. Looking back, I wonder if she knew what fate she was about to meet. We tussled our way up the stairs, but I won! I was so proud, and she looked amazing in my living room. Yup, I plopped her right in the windowless corner. I thought the light from the window way, way across the room would be enough. It was not. I proceeded to kill that plant so fast it made my head spin! I didn't even get a chance to pick out a decorative pot. Each day there was a fresh layer of dropped leaves. She went from full and lush to something that resembled that sad tree on the Charlie Brown Christmas special. It was swift, and, I hope, painless.

This convinced me that indoor plants just weren't my thing. I did not get that from my mama. I thought neither of my two thumbs were green. So I kept my plant love for outside. As soon as I had a yard of my own, I got to planting. There I found success, and I loved it. Much of the watering was handled by the rain.

I had no adult experience caring for indoor plants. But fast forward a few years, once Fiona came into my life and, instead of dying, began putting out new leaves, a switch flipped, and I wanted to know more. I figured if she was growing from just my watering, there were probably some other things I could do that would really make her thrive. I learned that she wanted bright light and to dry a bit between watering, and her leaves needed wiping so they'd be dust-free to photosynthesize. I also had to rotate her every now and then so that she didn't become lopsided—houseplants will actually grow toward the light. I thought that was just fascinating. I also needed to fertilize her when she was actively growing. The fertilizer "rabbit hole" was deep, and seemingly endless—I started with those gray plant spikes but later moved on to a diluted liquid fertilizer when she was actively growing. Turns out, there was way more to keeping her alive and happy than just watering!

I began checking on that one plant before doing anything else in the morning. And without planning, I suddenly had a new morning routine that was more than just checking the list of tasks that I had to do. Before I got into the emails, phone calls, and errands, I'd have my cup of liquid gold (aka coffee) and check on my plant. It was a few minutes of morning quiet that were all mine. I came to cherish those few minutes that I hadn't even realized I desperately needed. Checking her for new leaves and overall good health became my daily routine. I looked around and noticed all the well-lit places in my home that were begging for a plant or two. So, I decided to add a few more. I went from one plant to five—or was it ten? I don't know (remember my no counting rule!). At first this seemed like a lot, but I enjoyed it. Fiona had taught me it was more than just water, so, with the others, I deep dived into researching them and learned all that I could about their needs. I had something on the to-do list that I *enjoyed* doing, and it was just for me.

Fiona, my fiddle-leaf fig, established a morning routine for me that I have maintained to this day. Some moments of quiet with my coffee and checking on my plants are just the things I need to start the day with purpose rather than running on autopilot. Before my head fills with the chatter of "to dos" I like to daydream with my plants. Why do we stop daydreaming after we hit a certain age?

Can you start with that plant?

The *Ficus lyrata*, commonly known as the fiddle-leaf fig, has quite the reputation for drama. I can honestly say it is not entirely unwarranted. She can be quite the diva, but I think that is done only under protest, when her needs are not being met. Once you know this plant's care or needs and if you can provide them in your home, the fiddle-leaf fig makes quite the elegant statement plant.

- **Light.** Fiddle-leaf figs in nature are huge, tall trees that grow in full sun. That means that in your home, this plant is going to need very, very bright light. If you have unobstructed windows and you can see the sun in the sky when you look out of the window, this could be the plant for you. The aesthetic placement you will often see in magazines and on design shows has the statuesque fiddle-leaf fig gracing a windowless corner of a room. I'm willing to bet that plant is either fake or fresh from the nursery and hasn't had time to struggle yet. A fiddle-leaf fig will not survive in a windowless corner without the assistance of a grow light. You will want to place the plant close to the light source rather than across the room from it. It will grow toward the light, so if you care about a balanced look you will need to rotate the plant regularly. While its reputation for drama may be a little overstated, there is one thing that seems to be true of this plant. Once you establish a place in your home for it, and it likes it, you are going to want to just leave it there. The fiddle-leaf fig is not one of those plants that you can move around your home at your whim—believe me, I have tried with very unsuccessful results.

- **Water.** After the lighting demand is met, you'll find that less is more for watering this one. This plant does not like prolonged periods of moist soil. Allow the soil to dry between waterings. Grab a chopstick or plastic fork and aerate the soil so that there is good oxygen flow for the roots. This plant task is not one that you can do too often—so have at it and get to poking! She also benefits from a well-balanced nitrogen, phosphorus, and potassium (NPK) fertilizer when she is actively growing. Some plants do have a period of dormancy, especially during the winter months, where their growth slows substantially or even stops for a period. I have found that my plants in their temperature-controlled environment do not go fully dormant, so I fertilize year-round.

I started with this plant, but it is not one that would generally make it onto any beginner's list. If you start with a plant that is not traditionally recommended for first-time plant parents, have no fear. It is very possible to have success. The first step is to research the plant's needs and assess your indoor environment. This is true for any plant that you are caring for the first time.

The *Ficus lyrata*, also known as the fiddle-leaf fig, is not what anyone would call a "beginner plant," but life is full of surprises! This plant started my plant journey. While it has a reputation as a drama queen, with the right conditions anyone can grow this plant.

What are you feeding that plant?

When growing outdoors, plants have access to rich nutrients from their surrounding environment. When you grow plants indoors, they will need more than just plain water. To grow your plants full and lush you will need to add fertilizer to your plant-care routine. As a general rule, look for a fertilizer specifically formulated for indoor houseplants that provides the big three macronutrients—nitrogen, phosphorus, and potassium (NPK)—along with varying micronutrients. You do not want to use a fertilizer formulated for outdoor shrubs on your indoor houseplants. While there are fertilizers for specific houseplants, I like to keep things as simple as humanly possible. General houseplant fertilizers with a balanced NPK ratio absolutely get the job done. While the substance is the same, there are different forms of fertilizer to choose from. What you choose is really a matter of preference as they need to be applied with different frequencies.

- **Liquid fertilizer.** A liquid fertilizer comes in a concentrate that needs to be diluted with water. It is important to always follow the dilution instructions on the package when mixing.

- **Granular fertilizers.** These products do not require any mixing. You sprinkle them directly on the soil and water them in. Usually they need to be applied about once a month.

- **Slow-release fertilizers.** These plant foods come in little bead forms or spikes that you press down into the soil. Both will slowly release fertilizer into the plant every time you water. They have to be applied with the least frequency, approximately once every three or four months.

Whatever form of fertilizer you choose to use, it is important to follow package instructions for the amount to use and frequency of application. This is not something you want to try and wing, because you can damage your plants if the fertilizer is not mixed properly or you apply it too frequently. Plants need to be fertilized when the plant is actively growing.

CHAPTER 2

Save a Little Something for Yourself

Use Houseplants to Turn Borderline Burn-Out into Personal Growth.
Plus, the Best Plants to Get You Started

When you are giving so much of yourself to everything and to everyone, it's important to save a little something for yourself. This is, of course, sometimes much easier said than done. It is especially true if you are caring for someone other than yourself. And if that person is completely reliant upon you for all of their needs and wants, then it can feel particularly hard to do. When I would try to take a little time for myself, I was often riddled with feelings of guilt. Especially that mother guilt! It's a powerful emotion, but also entirely useless. Guilt serves no purpose other than to rob you of enjoyment. When I neglected myself in the service of appeasing that guilt, all I did was sow little tiny seeds of resentment and frustration. And that is not good for anyone. Just as you nurture your partner or spouse, your friends and family, you must also nurture yourself. One way to do this is to cultivate something you enjoy that is wholly your own and is leisurely. "Leisurely" is the part to focus on.

Popping into Larchmont Nurseries for a look around is one of my favorite things to do when I'm out running errands.

Self-Interest

Not only was I not on my "to-do lists," but if I made a list of the things that I enjoyed doing and compared it to my daily list of things to do, they simply did not line up. There was no overlap between the list of the things that I was doing and the list of things that I actually enjoyed doing. Something had to change.

We have been so conditioned to think that putting ourselves first and caring for ourselves is somehow selfish. It took some real intentional work for me to adjust that thinking, to turn it on its head. When I was good to myself, it made it so much easier to be good to others. It's just like the emergency instructions on an airplane before you take off into the friendly skies. The instructions are **not** to help your neighbor get their mask on and then put yours on. Quite the opposite, they tell you to put your mask on first and only then help others who are around you. It's a literal illustration of how helping yourself, taking care of yourself, helps you better care for others. And yet I know so many of us do not, or are hesitant to, apply this same reasoning in our day-to-day lives. What we have been conditioned to believe will take very intentional action and work to unlearn. Taking time for yourself is the same as putting on your own oxygen mask first.

I had to learn to also nurture myself, just as I nurtured my family, my friends, and my clients. I did that by leaning into a hobby that was wholly my own interest and also leisurely. Initially, my family could not have been less interested in my plants. And honestly, it's better that it started that way. It allowed me time to explore plants on my own and really delve into this interest at my own pace. More importantly, I was nurturing this interest free from groupthink. You know how when you are interested in something, but the rest of the group isn't, this can sometimes influence you and dampen your interest in it too? I hate when that happens. I once wanted to take a basket weaving class but let a group of friends convince me to try knitting instead. Now I have

a bag full of yarn and a half-finished scarf. I can't help but wonder if I'd be knee-deep in baskets right now if I had taken the basket weaving class instead. By flying solo, I did not face any of those risks. Plus, a "group interest" would have been like a family vacation.

A real vacation gives you a chance to reset and recharge your depleted battery. It gives you a chance to daydream and let your mind wander while you lie back in the warm air—preferably by the water with a frozen cocktail—and drift with the clouds. *That* is a vacation. But a family vacation is very different from that. On a family vacation there's the daily task of deciding what activity will make at least half of the group happy (it will never be the whole group, so it's better to just give up on that dream). And don't forget to adjust any schedule of family vacation activities to add in time for figuring out where to go when someone is hungry, bored, or needs to use the bathroom. Anyone who has ever been on a family vacation with kids knows it is not a real vacation. It is a trip with your family. And while it is also fun, it is very, very different from a real vacation. When we return home from a family trip, I am usually in desperate need of a vacation.

So, I coaxed and nurtured this newfound interest in indoor plants on my own and at my own pace. Besides having plants at home, I just enjoyed being around plants. I got a membership at a New York botanical garden and spent hours in the conservatory. But I didn't need a botanical garden to get my plant fix. It seems like these days everyone is in the business of selling plants. I sought them out at every store and took slow strolls browsing and leaf stroking. Most of my errands were planned around stopping at Larchmont Nurseries, a wonderful local nursery that had a huge greenhouse. But they didn't fill it with just rows of plants. Instead, they created an indoor tropical paradise complete with an enormous *Monstera deliciosa* that bore fruit, tall ficus trees draped with Spanish moss, and a small waterfall that fed into a koi pond. A koi pond! This is no ordinary nursery. When I can't make it to the botanical garden, this place does the trick!

Would you eat that?

Did you know the *Monstera deliciosa* produces edible fruit? I hadn't seen it in real life before visiting a favorite local nursery. It looks like something from the future—like an ear of corn wrapped in a sheath of neoprene ready to be sent into outer space. When I saw it in person, I had to deep dive down an internet rabbit hole and learn everything there was to know! Join me on this little word nerd trip. A mature *Monstera deliciosa* will produce what I've always called a flower but is actually called an inflorescence. The inflorescence has a silky, off-white spathe—the part that looks like a cup-shaped petal—that encloses a tall, white spadix. The spadix is the part that looks like a fleshy spike with a honeycomb pattern all over it. I learned that this honeycomb is not just a pattern, it's actually the tiny flowers. When these tiny flowers are fully pollinated, the spadix turns into the edible fruit. It will then scale over, and the scales drop off once the fruit is fully ripened. The flesh of the fruit is pale yellow and looks like kernels of corn. It is described as having a creamy texture, and the taste is said to be a cross between a pineapple and a banana. I'm fascinated but not daring enough to try it. The fact that this nursery has a *Monstera deliciosa* that produces fruit is no small feat. That usually only happens in a tropical environment outdoors. Need I remind you, this nursery is in Larchmont, New York, a decidedly not tropical environment! But when you step into their greenhouse, you are immediately transported to what feels and looks like an island paradise. The fruit is the only part of the *Monstera deliciosa* that is not toxic, but only if it is fully ripened. And this can take up to a year to achieve! Needless to say, I will happily enjoy watching it from afar! But I have tried the nectar from hoyas, and it's delicious (more on that later).

This is the *Monstera deliciosa* inflorescence and fruit. Before visiting Larchmont Nurseries, in Larchmont, New York, I had only seen pictures of the fruit online. It is said to be delicious, like a cross between a pineapple and a banana. Perhaps that is where its botanical name comes from!

This trailing moss is often sold in craft stores but is actually a living plant—*Tillandsia usneoides* is commonly known as Spanish moss. It is not actually moss but an epiphyte, or air plant, and it grows by hanging on trees and branches rather than in soil. It does not root onto the tree. Instead, it gets what it needs from rain and airborne particles. It's also not from Spain: Rather, it's native to Central America, Mexico, and southern regions of the US.

Visiting Larchmont Nurseries is like a quick trip to the botanical garden, and, while I have never tried the fruit of the *Monstera deliciosa*, the visits were and are food for my soul. That little seed that was planted by Fiona, the fiddle-leaf fig grew and grew. Suddenly, I had this new hobby that I felt very passionately about and was committed to. I could happily whittle away hours doing anything that involved plants—whether my own, or just ogling the ones on display. I'm not ashamed to admit that I spent many late-night hours scrolling and looking at plants online like some people look at porn, adding to my ever-growing and seemingly never-ending wish list of plants that I wanted. It was something I did just for the pure sake of leisure and enjoyment. At least that is what I initially thought about my small collection of ten plants. They were just something to whittle away the time with—a welcome distraction during a busy day, a brain break between emails and phone calls. But, as it turns out, it was actually much more.

In caring for my plants, I managed to put myself on my to-do list. There was finally overlap between the things to do list and the things I enjoyed doing list. I was intentionally carving out time to do something I enjoyed, just for me. More importantly, this plant thing was not in furtherance of a job, or volunteer project, or something for my family.

It is easy to get lost in the roles we have in our lives, whether it's the role of spouse, mother, partner, manager—whatever it is. But we are more than those roles and those titles. While we are all connected, we are also separate and unique beings with our own set of basic needs. Before I stepped into any of these roles, I was an individual person with my own interests and desires. Somewhere along the way I forgot about them. This new thing with houseplants reminded me of that. It was just for me. This quality alone time was thrilling! While I did not

start with what would be considered a beginner's plant, I knew my success with that plant was just sheer luck. I had no idea what I was doing, but I just did it anyway. Of course, it did not take long before I wanted to, and did, expand my collection. But more than just adding plants, I wanted to continue to build my confidence in growing houseplants. I wanted that indoor jungle, but to get that I had to learn how to keep these beauties alive.

Which Plants to Start With?

I had started with just one plant, but I wanted many more. In caring for that one plant, so many of the memories of my mother's indoor jungle came flooding back. I remembered how beautiful our small, plant-filled apartment was. I remembered how much enjoyment I found in helping my mother and watching her tend to her plants. Boston ferns are her favorite plant, and she had them hanging everywhere. I knew ferns were not the next step for me to add to my collection—I already had a few dead fern bodies buried out in the backyard. But I wanted to recreate a bit of that indoor jungle that I grew up with, so I circled back around to some fan favorites. Whether you are experienced or just beginning, these beauties are forgiving and loyal, and deserve a spot in any home.

Why hang fabric curtains when you can hang a plant curtain? One of my favorite ways to style plants is to hang a group of them in front of a window. Pro tip: Use a clothing rod instead of a curtain rod. It extends out farther from the wall, allowing room for more plants!

Pothos

Epipremnum aureum is from the Araceae family, and is native to southeastern Asia. Most *Epipremnum* go by the common name pothos, but they are also called devil's ivy. These are not your grandmother's plants. There is tremendous cultivar variety in this plant species, and the styling possibilities are endless. One of my favorites is the 'Manjula' pothos. Each individual leaf looks like a heart-shaped watercolor masterpiece of different shades of green and creamy white.

But if it's a solid-colored leaf that your heart desires, the silvery-bluish-greenish leaf of a similar species *Epipremnum pinnatum* 'Cebu Blue' will make you stop and stare for hours. To achieve the indoor tropical jungle vibe, you simply must include at least one pothos. In my humble opinion, it is the key ingredient. Have you ever seen a jungle without hanging vines? I haven't. You can let this beauty trail down from hanging planters, bookshelves, or floating shelves. I chase the light in my house, so there are floating shelves everywhere with a plant or two. Trailing is pretty standard for pothos grown indoors.

But you are not limited to hanging or trailing. You can really mix things up and turn a pothos into a beautiful floor plant. How, you ask? By adding a moss pole or an unfinished board or any type of pole for the plant to climb up.

Initially, you will have to give the plant an assist and attach it to the pole with coated floral wire or gardening Velcro tape. If you keep the pole or board moist, as the aerial roots develop, they will eventually begin to attach on their own and climb up the pole. In their natural habitat, these beauties are climbers and cling to the bark of tree trunks and work their way up. When you give yours something to climb, they'll reward you with enormous leaves! The leaves of very mature plants may even split and fenestrate, giving the plant a whole new look! When they are allowed to trail, you will notice that sometimes the plant develops leafless vines as it stretches and looks for something to climb. Just give those a trim until your plant is looking full and lush. I cannot decide which look I love more. Rather than choose, I have a combination of stylings throughout my home. Some trail, some climb—but all liven the décor in every room they grace.

Pothos generally like indirect, bright light. However, the more variegated types, like the 'Manjula' and 'Marble Queen', need bright light to maintain their beautiful coloring. They are very forgiving and will survive if you forget the next watering. They propagate easily in water or soil, making them great to share with friends or just to add more to your collection.

This is not your grandmother's pothos! There is such variety in this plant group. You can find everything from the solid dark green leaves of *Epipremnum aureum* 'Jade', to the painterly variegated leaves of 'Manjula' pothos, to the near white leaves of 'Snow Queen' pothos. And there are endless ways to incorporate them into your décor, not just as hanging plants. This 'Manjula' on a three-legged gold stand is a natural work of art and steals the show!

ZZ Plant

Zamioculcas zamiifolia is from the Araceae family, native to eastern Africa, and bears the common nickname of ZZ plant or the Zanzibar Gem. You can find this plant in either a glossy green version or a mysterious black version. Did your mouth just drop? Mine did too when I first learned of black plants. The new growth emerges a bright chartreuse green and slowly darkens to a glossy black.

Whether you choose the green or black version (or both), this beauty is the platinum standard of low maintenance plants. They have rhizomes, which are thick underground stems, that hold onto water. Thanks to these rhizomes, the ZZ plant is tolerant of drought and does not need to be watered often. That means it is quite forgiving if you take a long trip or just forget it for a while on that tall bookshelf. This may sound shocking, but I water mine only once every three to four weeks. It will thrive in bright, indirect light but is adaptable to many lighting conditions. The brighter the light, the faster this plant will send out tall shoots of new growth. The leaves can get quite large as the plant matures and can reach heights of three to four feet tall (1 to 1.2 m).

Another plus, ZZ plants prefer to be snug (but not rootbound) in their pot and do not need to be repotted often. You simply cannot go wrong with a ZZ plant. I love them so and have added many to my collection. You can propagate ZZ plants from stem or leaf cuttings or by division. If you go the route of starting cuttings, whether a leaf or stem, it is a long game and will take the patience of Job while waiting on the roots to develop.

Always bet on black! A black plant is simply a show-stopper. We know green. We know green and white. But black plants? Wow! *Zamioculcas zamiifolia* 'Dowon', commonly known as Raven ZZ plant, offers such depth and mystery. They are a must-have plant.

Snake Plant

The *Dracaena trifasciata* is from the Asparagaceae family, native to tropical regions in West Africa. I'm sure the first thing that comes to your mind when you hear "snake plant" is a boring office waiting room. They are a standard fixture in offices across the globe because they can tolerate the low levels of light from fluorescent bulbs. But don't be fooled by their corporate presence. These beauties are anything but boring!

There is tremendous variety in this plant family, with over sixty looks to choose from. Some snake plants are as small as six inches (15 cm), others as tall as six feet (1.8 m)! Some have twisted leaves; others are short and spikey. Some are nearly black and others are pale green with white stripes. The *D. trifasciata* are tall and statuesque and easy!

They are also like potato chips—with their ease of care, it will be hard to stop at just one. Like the ZZ plants, they have rhizomes that store water. They are very drought tolerant and adaptable to many different indoor lighting conditions and humidity. They are often described as low-light plants, because of their ability to tolerate lower lighting levels. But this plant in low light will not thrive. Don't expect to see much growth—or any— if you give a plant low light. And make no mistake, they will not survive in a windowless bathroom unless you plan on leaving the light on all day.

While some plant families have a bad rap for drama, this one is just the opposite. Some think snake plants are boring office plants, but I beg to differ! If it's a statuesque plant you want, this is the family for you. The *Dracaena* (formerly *Sansevieria*) *trifasciata* can grow up to 6 feet (1.8 m) tall! Those glossy blades and clean lines are perfect in settings with midcentury modern décor. These snake plants were found at Larchmont Nurseries.

Hoya

Hoyas are from the Apocynaceae (milkweed) family and are native to eastern Asia. This genus of plants was completely unknown to me before I started collecting plants. And baby, let me tell you now—I am obsessed!

The exact number is not known, but there are hundreds of different species of *Hoya*. The more popular species are typically kept as house-plants and are slow-growing, vining plants with thick, waxy leaves. But when I say their variety is endless, I really mean their variety is endless! Some hoyas have itty-bitty fuzzy leaves, others have leaves the size of dinner plates. They prefer a very chunky soil mix and to dry between watering. They can manage if you miss a watering or two. When they are really thirsty they will let you know they need a good drink because they get soft, wrinkled leaves. If you have the gift of bright, direct light, you will definitely want to add a hoya or two (or three or five or maybe even a few more) to your collection.

While you come for the foliage, you'll stay for the blooms. Hoya blooms are other-worldly.

They look like delicate confectionary flowers, crafted from marzipan or fondant frosting—something you might find dotted along a multi-tiered wedding cake or in a garden on Tatooine. Some blooms are perfectly spherical, while others look like shooting stars. They all secrete an edible nectar that tastes like something between simple syrup and honey. Yes, I've tasted the nectar, and I'm willing to bet you will too. The scent varies from very subtle and sweet to chocolate. Yes, chocolate!

Before collecting hoyas, I thought a new leaf on a plant was thrilling. Well, let me tell you—nothing compares to spotting a long-awaited peduncle (which is the name for the weird little nub that grows along the stem and produces the cluster of fuzzy blooms). Their growth pattern can be wild, and they do well when given a trellis to climb and wrap their tendrils around. Hoyas often send out leafless runners that they use to climb when in the wild. As a general rule of thumb, do not cut those runners. They eventually produce leaves, and more importantly, more peduncles!

Can I get a "hoyaaaa"? Once you add any single plant from this genus, you will be hooked (this one is *Hoya carnosa* 'Compacta'). You will not be able to stop at just one, because they are just delightful! Of all the plant discoveries I have made along this plant journey, this is probably my favorite. You'll add them for their foliage and obsess over them because of their otherworldly blooms!

Aglaonema

A member of the Araceae family, this genus is native to tropical regions of Asia and New Guinea. They are commonly known as the Chinese evergreen. In my humble opinion, this plant genus is highly underrated and isn't raved about nearly enough. They are spectacular!

You'll often spot huge pots of *Aglaonema* in indoor malls, offices, and hotel lobbies. Why? Because in nature they grow on the rainforest floor, under the canopy of larger plants. Therefore, they can flourish and thrive in artificial lighting alone. Add a window or two and they really take off, but these beauties do not need or want direct bright light.

If its variegation you seek, this is the plant for you. You can find them with leaves of green and white, pink and white, red and green, and different shades of green. There's even one with a spectacular sparkly camouflage-patterned leaf. Their lighting needs vary, depending upon the color of the leaf. Plants with loads of white or light-colored variegation will need more light. The green leaved varieties, if you are light challenged, do well in artificial light alone. Regardless of leaf color, they all adapt to average household humidity and can tolerate some drought.

The *Aglaonema* genus, commonly known as Chinese evergreens, is an excellent plant to add to any collection, no matter the level of growing experience. In this one plant, you can find a variety of leaf colors and patterns, from pink and white, to red and yellow, to green and white. There's even a sparkly camouflage leaf variety! The styling options are endless.

Monstera

A member of the Araceae family, this genus is native to Mexico. It is often mislabeled as a split-leaf philodendron—they are both from the same larger plant family but are two different plants. There are few plants that command as much attention or loyal fan following as the *Monstera deliciosa*. In my humble opinion, this is the must-have houseplant of all the plants.

While the entire family is pretty cool, the *Monstera deliciosa* 'Albo-Variegata' and the *Monstera deliciosa* 'Thai Constellation' are some of the most coveted plants. Monstera Peru (*Monstera karstenianum*), with its dark green bullate leaves, is also beautiful for its blister-like swellings. However, straight *M. deliciosa* is the plant that would I highly recommend for any collection and any level of growing experience. This is a showstopper plant, your centerpiece. This plant is a constant grower and shower. As the plant matures, the large, heart-shaped leaves develop fenestrations—which literally means openings or holes. Treat yourself to a larger specimen so that you get those huge fenestrated leaves right from the start. It can grow quite large and beautifully wild. You can stake it or prune it to control the shape, or hold off on frequently repotting it to keep some of that growth at bay. Stem cuttings root easily and are perfect for sharing with friends or for adding a monstera to every room. A cutting in a glass vase also makes quite a stunning table centerpiece.

The leaves of *Monstera deliciosa* are iconic. You can find this leaf pattern on everything from wallpaper, pillows, rugs, clothes, and more. If it is a large focal-point plant that you're after, this is the one for you!

DIY moss pole

So, you want to turn that vining plant into a climbing plant? You'll need a pole for that! You can use many things to stake your vining plant—an unfinished wooden board, garden stakes, bamboo poles, driftwood, or other materials. But my favorite is a DIY moss pole. Sure you can buy one, but where's the fun in that? They are easy to make, and you can customize them to an exact size for any plant. Here's the short list of supplies that you will need:

- Plastic container with lid
- Sphagnum moss
- PVC coated hardware (wire) mesh
- Heavy duty zip ties
- Velcro garden tape or coated floral wire
- Wire cutters
- Plastic drop cloth

Want to turn that hanging plant into a floor plant? All you need is a pole! You can make your own moss pole with a few simple supplies: moistened sphagnum moss, hardware mesh, and zip ties. When you make your own moss pole you can customize its size and shape. A climbing plant can make quite the design statement, as many will grow huge leaves when they are allowed to climb.

This project can get a little messy, so prepare your space with a plastic drop cloth before you get started if you are working indoors. After you gather up your materials, here's how to make your own moss pole.

1. Drop your dried sphagnum moss in the plastic container and add water. Cover and let it soak for at least an hour. Make sure your moss is fully rehydrated. I like to let mine soak overnight to really get the job done and leave no dry fibers. The amount of moss you use will depend upon the size of the pole you are making.

2. Cut your hardware mesh to the size you would like. A good formula to follow is to cut a piece at least 12 inches (30 cm) taller than the plant you are using, plus the depth of the planter you are potting in. Lay the hardware mesh out flat on your work surface to measure. Once cut, shape the hardware mesh into a round cylinder shape or fold the sides in to shape it like a tamale. This is simply a matter of preference. Both the cylinder and tamale shapes get the job done. For a cylinder, you do not need a large diameter—2 to 3 inches (5 to 8 cm) works well. The bigger the pole, the heavier it will be in the pot and the harder to keep moist.

3. Arrange the moistened sphagnum moss in the middle of the hardware mesh. For this job, more is more. You do not want to skimp on the moss. Make sure you have enough to pack it firmly when you close up the hardware mesh as the moss will loosen over time, so start by making it tight! As you are filling the open mesh, press out the excess moisture to ensure that the moss will be tightly packed. Remember that plastic drop cloth I mentioned? You'll want to make sure that it is in place before you start pressing out the water. Don't be like me and realize it's still folded on a chair after you start pressing away! Leave a little of the mesh empty on the end that will go into the pot.

4. After you have filled the center of the mesh with moistened sphagnum moss, it is time to close up the sides. Bring both sides of the mesh together so that they overlap. Grab a zip tie and insert it into the overlapping squares to lock them together. Pull the zip tie tightly to secure it. Repeat this step up the length of the pole, at 1- to 2-inch (2.5 to 5 cm) intervals. After it is closed, you can trim the excess off the zip ties for a cleaner look.

5. When adding the pole to your planter, start with an empty one. It will be easier to position. Place the moss pole smack in the center of the empty planter. You can add pebbles around the bottom of the pole to help add weight to the planter so that it is not top heavy.

6. When adding the plant, you have the choice of adding an established plant or using freshly rooted cuttings (see the image on the next page for my thoughts on this). Either way, you will need to initially give the plant an assist and secure it to the pole with the Velcro tape or the coated floral wire. The Velcro tape will be easier to take off and reposition if you need to. Make sure that the aerial roots of the plant are firmly touching the moss pole. The plant will eventually climb on its own using its aerial roots, so making sure they touch is important.

7. There is much debate about whether or not you need to keep the pole moist for the plant to attach. Based upon my experience, I've never had a plant successfully attach without keeping the pole moist, especially at the point of contact with the aerial roots. To moisten the pole, you can mist it regularly or pop a watering globe into the top of the pole.

The *Scindapsus pictus* 'Exotica' is a beautiful choice for a moss pole. When this plant is allowed to climb, those silvery leaves become enormous. Pro tip: Instead of staking an established plant, use freshly rooted cuttings. As they grow, they will attach to the moss pole more quickly on their own.

53

Expanding Your Collection for Free!

So, you have begun your plant parent journey and found some plants that you really like, and they like you back. There is nothing wrong with having doubles (triples even), but you don't have to buy them. There is a way to get more plants for free, and it's even more exciting than plant shopping—it's propagating. Propagating is the magical act of cloning your plants to make more plants! There are many methods of propagating. Here are just a few of my favorites.

WATER

My very favorite tried-and-true method for propagating is in water. Why? Mostly because I am nosey and like to watch the roots develop on the cuttings. It's very hard to check the progress of root development when you can't see the roots. Pothos, monstera, philodendron, and coleus root well in water, but more woody plants will probably sulk and rot.

I also love using this method to propagate because a cutting rooting in water can be very beautiful. In the right vessel, it makes the perfect centerpiece for the table. Next are some reliable tips I use for success when propagating in water.

- **Get the right cut.** Along the stem of a plant, you'll find nodes. Nodes contain the blueprint for the new plant that will eventually develop after the cutting is rooted. Without a node, the cutting may produce roots, but it will never be a new plant. It will be what is called a "zombie leaf." Most of those cute heart-shaped *Hoya kerrii* they sell around Valentine's day are zombie leaves. Nodes are always located at the base of where a leaf meets the stem. Some nodes are easy to spot, even when there is no leaf, because the stem will be slightly protruded or fatter in the spot where the node is. The key to success is always making the correct cut on your cutting—just below the node. Without the node, the cutting will not develop new leaves.

Of course, there are a few exceptions. Some plants, like *Peperomia*, can be rooted with just a cutting from the stem or even from a single leaf. Others, like snake plants, can also be rooted with leaf cuttings. The key here is still in the cut. You want to cut the stem on a 45-degree angle or the leaf into a *V* shape so that the cutting does not sit flush against the bottom of the vessel. This will help prevent the cutting from rotting and turning to mush.

Also, remember to remove any lower leaves (you do not want to submerge any leaves in water they will turn to mush too).

- **Use a small container.** The cuttings will secrete small amounts of hormones into the water as it is slowly developing roots. The smaller the vessel or container, the more available the hormones will be in the water. You do not need a gallon-sized jug full of water to root a cutting.

- **Less is more.** Just as a small container is better, the same is true for the amount of water you root in. You need just enough to completely cover the node and aerial roots (when they are there), and to keep the bottom of the cutting well submerged in water. Keep an eye on the cutting and add more water as the water level drops. Refresh the water if it starts to get cloudy and gross. This is important to keep oxygen in the water and to keep it free from bacteria that can cause stem or root rot.

- **Let there be light.** Place the cutting in an area that gets the ambient light from the room. There is no need to place the cutting in direct light (besides, this could lead to algae growth in the water). The focus is on root development.

You can add plants to your collection without buying more plants! One of the most rewarding things you can do with your plants is make more plants from the ones you already have! You can propagate to add plants to your collection, or to make your small plant look fuller faster. There are many different methods of houseplant propagation but rooting in water remains my favorite.

This *Monstera deliciosa* cutting rooting in water makes for a stunning table centerpiece. While the vessel is tall, there is just enough water to cover the nodes and aerial roots. You do not need to fill the container to the top when rooting in water. But you do need to top up the water when it evaporates to replenish oxygen for the roots. The cutting will also secrete a small amount of hormones that help it develop roots. The less water there is, the more concentrated the hormones and the faster the rooting process.

- **Got roots?** Roots can take a few weeks to develop, so do not get discouraged if you don't have roots after an hour or two. Of course, I'm kidding; you know it will take longer than an hour. But even with this knowledge, it's hard not to check on the cutting constantly. Trust me, I know. When you have roots that are 2 to 3 inches (5 to 8 cm) long, you are ready to transfer your cutting to soil. Do not transfer the cutting before the roots are well established. I have had more than one rooted cutting not make it because I planted it up too soon. Once in the soil, you have yourself a new plant! You can transfer the rooted cutting to its own pot or add it back to the original pot to make your mother plant look fuller faster. When potting up a rooted cutting in its own planter, it is always better to err on the side of small when it comes to choosing a planter. The roots are still developing, and you don't want to smother them in soil in a planter that is too big. Initially, you will want to make sure to keep the soil moist until you see that first sign of a new leaf. When a new leaf emerges, you know your cutting is now a fully established new plant.

SOIL

While this method is not nearly as much fun to watch, it is another reliable propagation method. The best part? You will not have to transfer the cutting because you are rooting directly in soil in a small planter—again the smaller the better. Here are some tips for success:

- **Water.** While you may not be rooting in water, it still plays a very important part when rooting in soil. The first step you want to take is to thoroughly hydrate the soil in the planter. When rooting in soil, it's a good idea to premoisten the soil to make sure the cutting gets adequate moisture. When I am propagating directly in soil, I really drench the soil and allow it to sit for at least thirty minutes to fully absorb the water.

- **Make the cut.** Like rooting in water, be sure to make the right cut and get a node on your cutting. Remove any lower leaves. You do not want to bury them in the soil. Bury the cutting in the soil, just above a node and below the remaining leaves.

- **Cover it up.** When rooting in soil, the cutting will need increased humidity. The best way to achieve this is to cover it. Plastic containers like salad clamshells and Ziploc bags do the trick. Drop the entire cutting and its pot inside and close it up.

- **Light.** Bright light is the final piece necessary for success. When rooting in soil, you'll need more than just the ambient light in the room. Place the cutting in a bright and warm area, cross your fingers, and wait. You can kick it up a notch by placing the pot onto a heated mat typically used for growing seedlings. They are also great for propagating in soil, especially in colder regions. It may be hard, but try and resist the temptation to open the plastic container and check on the cutting. Every time you open the container and peek, you are reducing the humidity.

AIR LAYERING

If you want to propagate, but are afraid to totally cut off a piece of the plant, then air layering is the method for you! You can root a whole new plant while the stem is still attached to your existing plant. There's no need to cut anything off until roots have formed. Once the roots have formed nicely along the stem, you cut off that part of the stem and pot it up. Plants propagated by this method often reach a big, lush size sooner than the other propagation methods, which often result in only putting out small leaves initially. Next are some tips for successful air layering.

- **Moss, moss baby.** For this method you will need moistened sphagnum moss. This is the medium that will be used to help the plant develop roots on the stem while the plant grows. Sphagnum moss is a dried plant that can be used for many things in the plant-care world. It is highly absorbent and retains moisture. This is what makes it great for propagating. Before beginning, you'll want to prepare the moss by fully rehydrating it. Sphagnum moss expands when it is rehydrated, so you do not need much of the dried product to begin with. When water is added, be sure to give it enough time to soak up the water fully. To really kick things up, you can add a little diluted liquid fertilizer to the water you are using to moisten the moss.

- **It's still all about the node.** Find a spot along the stem with at least one node. If you are air layering a plant that also develops visible aerial roots, like any philodendron or monstera, this is also a great place to wrap with moss.

- **Mark your spot.** When you have found the nodes or aerial roots, you're going to completely cover the area with well-moistened sphagnum moss. To keep it moist, you'll then need to cover the moss. I've seen all sorts of clever contraptions used to do this—cupcake containers, a Tupperware container with a hole cut in it, Starbucks cups, etc. I like to keep it simple and simply wrap it with old fashioned plastic food wrap. Secure the plastic-wrapped moss clump with twine or Velcro gardening tape, but not too tightly. When they have formed, the roots will need oxygen.

- **When you have roots.** You'll remove the cutting once the roots have developed in the moss. One of the qualities of sphagnum moss is its airiness. You will be able to see the roots through the plastic when they have reached a good length. Once they are clearly visible, you'll remove your cutting. Use a pair of pruners to cut off the stem just beneath where the roots have formed so your new cutting has a part of the stem and some leaves along with the roots. Don't worry about removing all of the moss from the roots before you pot up the cutting. It will not harm the plant or inhibit growth when you transfer the rooted cutting to soil. As an added plus to the method, you'll get new growth at the cut point on the mother plant!

MORE PROPAGATION TIPS

No matter the method of propagating, there are a few enhancements you can use to help speed up the rooting process for your cutting.

- **Hormone rooting powder.** This powder or liquid contains growth hormone rooting auxins and can be purchased at most gardening stores. You can apply it to the cut end of the cutting or, if air layering, dampen a small paint brush and brush it on the node and aerial root before wrapping it with damp moss. You can use rooting hormone when rooting in any medium.

- **Ceylon cinnamon.** When rooting in soil, Ceylon cinnamon is great for helping to speed up root develop and to help prevent the cutting from rotting.

- **Honey.** This came as the biggest surprise when I first started experimenting with propagating plants. Admittedly, I was quite dubious, but I gave it a try and successfully rooted my cuttings. You'll want to use raw honey, not the honey in the little plastic bear. Boil 2 cups (473 ml) of water and add 2 tablespoons (30 ml) of raw honey. Allow the mixture to cool before you dip your cutting in it. This can be used with any rooting medium.

Succulents are so much fun to propagate! All you need is a leaf. You gently twist the leaf off, allow it to dry for a day or two, and then lay it on top of soil. That's it! It's pure plant magic. Within no time, you can expand your collection.

CHAPTER 3

Water Yourself

Houseplant Cultivation Tips That Also Cultivate YOU

What do I mean by "water yourself"? Hydrate, literally. Most of us are walking around completely dehydrated wondering why our brain feels foggy and our energy is so low. If you are anything like I used to be, you carry that water bottle around like it is an emotional support animal. I never left home without it. When I headed out, I grabbed my keys, purse, phone, and water bottle—in that order. It would ride along with me wherever I went, my loyal passenger. If I had that nagging sensation of forgetting something, I promise you it was never my water bottle. We were attached at the hip. But was I actually drinking it? Well, you already know the answer to that. I cannot count the number of times that I told my children to drink more water, that their bodies needed water for every function, that they'd feel better if they were well hydrated. But I did not practice what I preached.

Most days, I would return home with that water bottle just a few sips shy of full. So, then I'd carry it around the house, from room to room. It sat on the desk or counter and kept me constant company as I worked. Its ever presence was comforting. Again, caring for others but not giving myself the same care. Rarely did I take my own advice and drink the water that was always at my side. I had my water bottle, but I always reached for that cup of coffee instead. Not because I thought it would quench my thirst, but because I thought it would give me some much-needed energy to push through to the next "to do." And if I'm being completely transparent, despite knowing the benefits of water, I like coffee better. No, I love it. I love coffee. I could drink it all day. I often did, in place of water or a meal, even. When I felt a slump in energy or felt a bit foggy, I had another cup of coffee. I never thought I should reach for water instead. And let's be clear, the coffee did not always give me the jump I needed, but I never changed the behavior.

But with plants, I had a living, visual aid—something to show me just how much living things need water to be their very best. When plants are thirsty, they wilt and droop; they become dry and brittle. Well, as it turns out, so too do I. While I don't water my plants every day—there are only a few types of plants that need that much water—I am constantly checking on them to see if they need watering. This regular water check-in for my plants has changed my relationship with my water bottle. It is no longer there just to keep me company. I actually drink from it now. It's hard to give my drooping plant water and simultaneously ignore my own need for a drink of water. The simple act of watering myself—making sure I down those ten (or more) glasses of water each day, has boosted my mood, energy, and completely brightened my complexion. Who doesn't want that?

It's Not Just Water

It is the act of POURING into yourself (you see what I did right there?). When you pour into yourself, you meet your own needs. Now, you might ask, "Who doesn't know that?" Of course, I knew that, but I didn't always practice what I preached.

When I was preaching, it was usually in the service of taking care of others. Which is who I have always been. You know how some kids have old souls? That was me. My mom and dad met when they were just thirteen years old and married when they were eighteen. My dad died when I was very young, and it was just my mom and me for many years before she remarried. Even though I was just a kid, my response was to comfort my mom—I hated seeing her sad. And that practice of comforting others, always trying to fix things and to make people happy, was a pattern of behavior that has continued throughout my life. That quest will keep you busy, very busy, and often times exhausted. If something was not going quite right for someone I loved and cared about, I kicked into high gear trying to find a way to fix it. I became very good at solving problems for others, while sweeping my own issues and needs to the side. It was very easy to brush off the fact that I was ignoring my own issues when I was busy helping others. I wanted to finish whatever it was I was working on, and get it crossed off the list. I rationalized to myself that I would get to my own list when I finished helping whomever or whatever project I had set my sights on.

I knew I needed to take inventory and change some bad habits—like skipping a decent meal and then eating junk because I was starving. But it was easier to keep powering through tasks and managing other peoples' bad habits rather than address my own. I had no time to stop. I had things to do and no time to stop and think about what I needed. I just had to get things done.

Water pouring down the leaf of a *Philodendron burle-marxii*. Water is life! Just as your plants need to stay hydrated, so do you. The same way they perk up when they are well hydrated, so do we!

How much happier would we be, if we all just paused with our plants? When I see my "framily" running like they are on a hamster wheel, I buy them a plant to help them hit the pause button.

This is what I would tell myself. But avoidance did not make anything that I pushed aside go away. It was nonsense, but I convinced myself it made perfect sense. I thought I would catch up on my own needs once I was finished handling the business of the day. I thought I would, but by the time "finished" rolled around it was evening, and time for wine and mindless television.

I was on autopilot and not taking the time to pay much attention. I felt mostly fine, so I did not notice, at first, how many of my most basic needs were being neglected. How often do you pause for a moment and check in on how you are truly feeling physically? And not just physically but also mentally? I wasn't doing that nearly enough. Instead, I would just push through the tired and the fog and keep going. After all, I had set up everyone to believe I could just keep going. That I was always fine, not ever feeling burned out or like I just needed a break.

But it wasn't just other people. I'd also applied that pressure to myself. Whether I was working for a client, taking care of my family, or volunteering, I wanted that sense of completion. The temporary euphoria of a job well done masked my other shortcomings. Around three o'clock I'd hit a slump and suddenly realize I had not had a morsel to eat and nary a drop of water to drink. I would chastise myself, promising to do better. And I would do better for a week or two, maybe even a month. Then I would slip right back into my usual bad behavior—habits are hard to break, even bad ones. It was a vicious cycle. How could I be at my best, or feel my best, if I was operating on fumes?

As much as I love coffee (it is liquid gold), no amount of caffeine can overcome exhaustion. And while I'd love for it to be so, I'm here to tell you—coffee is not a meal. Even if you load it up with cream and sugar. It just isn't. So, I had to make some purposeful and intentional changes. The ripping and running and neglecting myself was not sustainable, and it was beginning to really catch up with me. I had to slow down.

That is exactly what my plants helped me do. It was my daily routine of checking on them— whether they needed a drink, or to be rotated, or simply to say hello—that helped me. That check in made me pause. In that pause, I checked in on myself, too. What did I need? How was I feeling? At first, it felt a little hokey because it was not

something that I was used to. It was not my usual pattern of behavior, but when I sat down and really examined it, my usual pattern of behavior was not good for anyone. I had to get real and honest with myself. Sometimes I wasn't even delivering my best work because I was so tired and frustrated, and at times even a tiny bit resentful. I was both flattered that I was frequently on the short list of people to ask but also resentful because who was on *my* short list?

I needed help sometimes, too, but the help I needed I was already giving to someone else. I had myself boxed into a corner. I don't know how I had gotten it into my head that I was obligated to do all of those things, that I had some sort of duty to fulfill to everyone but myself. But now I had plants. I was going to have to hit the pause button on something so that I could take care of them. In hitting that pause button for them, I hit it for myself. My plants helped me be more intentional and consistent in checking on myself and taking care of my own basic needs. This small act made me feel so much happier, and it trickled down into many aspects of my life, not just my water consumption.

Slowing down to focus on my plants made me slow down, pause, and recharge. I can honestly say I'm not sure that I would have, without the intervention from my plants. Looking back, I do not see a path that would have lead me here, to this point in my life. In my life as it was, there was a longing for something more, but I did not carve out the time to stop to figure out what the "what" was. I convinced myself that I had to stay busy, and that being busy was enough, being a wife was enough, being a mother was enough. Until it wasn't. I did not feel like I had any one thing that I did for myself that made me feel fulfilled in a way that my other roles did not. I'm sure I'm not alone in this thinking. I look around every day and see people just running to and fro, on autopilot. I want to stop them, and hand them a plant.

So, you want to hang with your plants, but you don't want to drown them?

Overwatering is the most common mistake, for growers of all experience levels. There are many ways to kill a plant, but I'm willing to guess overwatering is the number one killer of plants. Soil holds onto moisture longer than we initially realize. As the result, plants don't need watering nearly as often as people think. But I get it, most times when we pick up the watering can it is just because we want to hang out with our plants without being empty handed and just standing there talking to them. I know I'm not the only one who does this. I used to feel slightly embarrassed when someone would shout from the other room, "You talking to me?" No, not you. I'm talking to the plants. I'm no longer embarrassed, and they no longer ask. You might not be there yet. But put down the watering can anyway. There are many tasks you can do instead of watering when you want to spend time with your plants.

We have to be the literal wind and rain against our plants' leaves, to help them stay dust-free. In nature, their leaves would get a good cleaning with every strong breeze and rainy day. Without the wind and the rain, we have to clean our plant leaves. This simple task helps them photosynthesize and helps us develop the good habit of regularly checking for uninvited guests (pests!).

- **Clean your plant's leaves.** In nature, plants have the rain and the wind to keep their leaves dust- and dirt-free so they can soak up all that good light and photosynthesize. In your home, you have to do the job of the rain and wind and keep those leaves clean. Dust can clog the plant's stomata. Stomata are tiny, pore-like openings mostly found on plant leaves but sometimes also on stems. The opening and closing of these tiny pores is needed for gas exchange. The plant is dependent on properly functioning stomata to photosynthesize and convert light into the energy that is needed to grow and produce those little new leaves. Keeping the leaves clean and dust-free, not only does this help them photosynthesize and look great, but it also gets rid of any tiny pests lurking around, waiting for their chance to wreak havoc. Many plant pests hang out on the underside of leaves, so cleaning the leaves also helps manage certain pests. Also, some pests, like the dreadful spider mites, are literally the worst and are very hard to rid your plant of. But they can be thwarted by staying on top of your pest watch. So, grab something soft and get to wiping those leaves.

- **Aerate soil.** This is probably the most underrated plant task and is weirdly satisfying to do. Grab an old pair of chopsticks or a skewer and give that soil a few jabs. Soil can become crusted and compacted over time. This can cause a few problems. The obvious one being that when the soil is compacted, it reduces the airflow to the roots. But also, when you water your plant and the soil is compacted, the water can go right down the sides of the planter and out the drainage hole, instead of soaking into the soil. That is why sometimes it can seem like the plant is still thirsty despite having just been watered. Your plant's roots need moisture and oxygen to flourish. Loosening the soil will increase airflow and help the water be more evenly distributed throughout the soil. All of this translates to more growth. Aerating the soil is something you can do as often as you want with wanton abandon! I've never heard it said that potting soil can be overaerated.

- **Trim and toss.** If you haven't already, trim and toss those yellowed leaves. They may drop on their own, but you don't want to leave them to decay in your planter. Certain pests and diseases are attracted to decaying plant tissue. When old leaves are allowed to remain in the pot and decay, you're potentially sending out an open invitation to very unwanted consequences.

- **Check for pests.** No one ever wants to ask the question they don't really want the answer to. The same is true when it comes to looking for pests. You may not want to check for pests for fear of spotting them, but you simply must!

The sooner you know, the sooner you can do something about it. Pests are inevitable when caring for plants indoors. But have no fear, most are manageable if spotted and caught early and will not spread to the other plants. The key is consistency in checking and dealing with the problem as soon as you spot it.

- **Rotate them.** Plants are phototropic. This means they will grow and stretch toward the light. It's quite fascinating and sometimes funny to watch how they stretch and lean toward the light. My *Alocasia* 'Regal Shields' practically knocks the planter over stretching toward the window. Without rotating it, all I see is the underside of the leaf. Take a look around and see who needs rotating. Some plants will need a full turn, others just a small adjustment to help the other side catch up to the side that was hogging all of the good light. This small act will help them stay evenly lush on all sides.

The next time you order takeout, don't toss those chopsticks! They are perfect for aerating the soil. Aerating loosens the soil, allowing oxygen to flow more freely around the roots. The soil in this *Anthurium pedatoradiatum* (also known as fingers anthurium) planter felt pretty compacted and needed aerating.

69

Overwatering is frequency, not volume

To avoid overwatering, you must first understand what overwatering is. It is the frequency of watering, not the volume of water, that leads to overwatering. When you are watering your plant, you want to fully rehydrate the soil. To do this, water the plant until the excess comes through the drainage holes. Do not water the plant again until it has had time to use up the moisture. In other words, for most houseplants, let the soil dry before watering again. A few signs your plant is ready to be watered again are:

- The plant pot feels lighter—dry soil weighs less than wet soil.

- The leaves are drooping or, for some plants like hoyas and succulents, the leaves will feel soft and look slightly wrinkled.

- Your moisture meter tells you so.

Check for those signs before watering. Ignore the advice on some of those plant care cards about watering when the top 1 to 2 inches (2.5 to 5 cm) of soil are dry. That's not nearly deep enough to tell you whether or not the plant needs watering, unless it is a very small plant. Imagine checking only the top 1 to 2 inches (2.5 to 5 cm) of soil on a plant in a 6-inch (15 cm) planter. Those planters are 6 inches (15 cm) in diameter and 6 inches (15 cm) in depth. The top 2 inches (5 cm) of soil will tell you little about what you need to know about the soil down where the roots are. There is usually still plenty of moisture deep in the pot when that top soil layer is dry.

Sometimes you just want to take the guesswork out of the equation. That's where a moisture meter come in. This handy little doohickey will let you know if the soil is still moist deep down in the planter by the roots. But don't leave it in the plant! It's like an oven thermometer— get the reading, and then get it out.

Got pests?

Having an occasional pest (or two or three) is pretty much par for the course when you are caring for houseplants. But don't panic, most are very easy to manage or get rid of. For a few, though, you'll want to dropkick the plant and pests right into the garbage can and bleach anything the plant may have touched. Here are some tips for the easily managed buggers:

FUNGUS GNATS

These are the most common houseplant pest. I'd be willing to bet if you asked every single person who has ever cared for plants, they will all say they've had fungus gnats. If they say they haven't, trust me, those gnats will make an appearance soon enough. Fungus gnats are the direct result of having soil that is moist for too long. How they spontaneously appear when the soil is wet too long, well that is something I will never ever understand. Besides organic matter and plant roots, they eat a fungus that thrives in moist potting soil. Here are the fixes to get rid of fungus gnats.

1. **Dry it out.** The first easy and obvious fix is to let the soil dry out as much as you can stand. Try to go past that next watering, and then go a few more days past that. Let the plant droop a little—just get that soil dry. Fungus gnat larvae cannot survive in dry soil. After you let the plant dry out, keep the top layer of soil dry by watering from the bottom. To bottom water, fill a container with water and drop the potted plant in it and let the plant soak it up. The dry soil will absorb the water from the bottom and the top layer of soil will remain dry, preventing adult fungus gnats from laying their devil-spawn eggs.

2. **Add a topdressing.** As an added preventative measure, cover the top of the soil with horticultural sand. The sand will both prevent the adult gnats from laying eggs in the soil and act as a barrier, smothering and trapping the larvae which may already be in the plant soil. Horticultural sand or coarse sand is preferred because it does not hold moisture.

3. **Ceylon cinnamon.** Now that you've rid yourself of them, you want to take measures to prevent the gnats from coming back. Ceylon cinnamon is a natural fungicide. Sprinkle the top of the soil generously to kill the fungus the gnats feed on and to repel any lingering adult gnats.

4. **Sticky traps.** After you've dried out the soil, catch any adults that may still be disturbing the peace and flying about with yellow sticky traps. Stick the traps right into your pots and they will attract the adults that tried to hide out in the other room while you were sprinkling sand and cinnamon on the soil. The adults are the literal worst! They are attracted to the CO_2 we expel every time we open our mouths to speak or laugh. There is nothing worse than a fungus gnat buzzing right up into your face while you're trying to watch a little television. The sticky traps come in cute shapes—I'm using that word loosely here—like butterflies and Yoda, making them just a little less gross and unsightly. They are a means to an end. Toss the sticky traps as soon as you catch the adults. No one wants a reminder of the hell you just lived through.

5. **Clean saucers.** After you've done all of the above things, here's the last thing you have to do to really rid your life of bitch-ass fungus gnats: Clean your dirty plant saucers. Fungus gnats are attracted to moist, decaying organic matter. While lots of initial moisture and decaying matter can be found in overwatered plants, they can set also up their basecamp in other dirty, stagnant areas. So, wash your plant saucers with some bleach or hot, soapy water when you've had a fungus gnat issue.

Fungus gnats can't infest plants if they can't get into the soil. You can throw a monkey wrench in their plans if you give your soil a topdressing of sand. Sand does not hold moisture, which fungus gnats need to nest and lay their devil-spawn eggs.

This *Rhaphidophora decursiva* had pesky fungus gnats that had overstayed their welcome. After letting it dry completely, I switched to exclusively bottom watering this one. By watering from the bottom, the top layer of soil remains dry and inhospitable to those pesky fungus gnats!

When you spot that first mealybug—and at some point you will—it can cause quite a panic. But keep calm and swab on! Whip out the rubbing alcohol and cotton swabs and get dabbing. They are an annoying pest but a manageable one.

MEALYBUGS

You ever see what looks like little white cottony stuff on a plant? That's not cotton, it's mealy-bugs. While these critters do not fly, they crawl and are equally annoying. When you spot them, you want to immediately quarantine the plant and inspect all of the plants that the infected one was near.

- **Blame it on the alcohol.** You'll want to grab some alcohol—rubbing, not drinking, that is—to get rid of these. Dip cotton balls and cotton swabs in rubbing alcohol and get at the mealybugs directly. They will die instantly. Then wipe and remove them. But don't stop there. Mix ½ to ⅔ cup (118 to 158 ml) of rubbing alcohol with 1 teaspoon (5 ml) of castile soap and 1 quart (946 ml) of water. Pour the mix into a spray bottle and test the spray mixture on a small, inconspicuous spot on your plant, wait 24 hours to see if there's damage to your plant (ferns and other thin leaf plants may be damaged by the spray). If there's no damage, douse the entire plant—tops and bottoms of leaves and the soil. Continue the spray treatment once a week for 2 to 3 weeks.

SCALE

These scabby-looking pests are related to mealybugs and are equally gross to remove—but remove you must. These pests look like tiny, usually oval-shaped crusty patches on your plants. Follow the same mealybug steps to remove and rid your plants of them.

SPIDER MITES

These are the White Walkers of plant pests—hard to kill, feared by most, and the cause of lots of destruction. If you spot spider mites on your plant, you will have a decision to make immediately—dropkick it into the trash or try and treat it. Don't want to toss it? Okay, but you will need to act really fast because the mites spread easily, and trust me, you DO NOT want that. Spider mites are awful, but you can sort of annihilate them and reclaim your peace. I've done it a couple times, and I lived to tell the tale. They tend to come back or were never truly gone. Spider mites first reveal themselves as what appears to be dust on your plant leaves—see why it's so important to stay on top of that regular cleaning? I digress, but that's the first sign—dusty leaves. The next sign will make you quake with fear—the appearance of fine webbing. If you see webbing, you're going to need dragonglass and some pretty intense miticides—some of which you can only find on the very dark web (kidding/not kidding).

- **Shower.** Your first line of defense is to shower the plant, but not just using any laidback shower. You're going to need to give it a shower with pressure á la Meryl Streep in *Silkwood* or Kramer in that *Seinfeld* episode where he bought the illegal high-pressure shower heads. Are any of these references reaching you? In simpler terms, you're going to need to give your plant a very forceful shower blast to knock off those vermin. You'll need to hit the plant from every direction—from the bottom to the top, make those mites drop.

- **Chemical warfare.** Here's where it gets really tricky. Spider mites are not insects, so insecticidal treatments will not always be effective. They'll see you coming with that bottle of insecticidal soap mix, and they'll laugh at you. You can "manage" spider mites with insecticides, and what I mean by that is, you can reduce their numbers and make them less visible. But you will not rid your plant of spider mites with insecticides—even if the packaging claims so. You'll need a miticide and an internet search for that. If you find a commercially available miticide in your area, buy extra and keep it on hand. Be sure to follow the label instructions carefully because you'll be using a chemical pesticide inside of your home.

- **Prevention.** Your best line of defense is prevention. There are some plants that are true spider mite hoes—like alocasia and calathea. You may want to avoid adding these plants to your collection. I found this out too late and had already fallen deeply and madly in love with an *Alocasia × amazonica* 'Polly' and a few *Calathea orbifolia*. It's too late for me. I take my chances with every purchase, but I have been able to avoid the mites' return by staying vigilant and keeping those two away from all of my other plants.

This list of pests is not exhaustive, but these are the fairly common pests most plant parents encounter at some point in their plant parenting journey. If you spot them, stay calm and treat away.

The best way to manage pests is to stay vigilant! Inspect your plants frequently with a magnifying glass. If you want to get super-duper fly and impress everyone you know, grab a jeweler's loupe. Be warned, that level of magnification on a mealybug is not for the faint of heart!

Make them shine like the top of the Chrysler Building!

Forget the store-bought leaf shine products and mayonnaise. This multiuse solution is all you'll need. Sure you can simply clean your plant's leaves with a soft dry cloth, but adding this mix to the task takes it up a notch. When it is time to clean my plants, I use a solution of water, peppermint castile soap, and neem oil. I mix 1 quart (946 ml) of water with 1 teaspoon (5 ml) of castile soap and ½ teaspoon (2.5 ml) of neem oil. This solution cleans the plant and gives the leaves a beautiful natural shine. Commercial leaf shine products can build up on the leaves and give them an artificial plasticky look. And mayonnaise? Well, that is just all kinds of wrong.

As a plant parent, these are the two of the hardest working liquids you'll ever meet. Castile soap (left) and neem oil (right) are two multipurpose power-houses! They are my go-to products for managing pests and keeping my plants looking their absolute dust-free best!

New Plant Parent Starter Pack

So, you have your new plants, and like any new parent, you want to give your new "babies" what they need. There are loads of gadgets marketed for indoor plant care and houseplant tools out there that you can add to your plant parent routine—some more useful than others. You'll find what works for you in your environment and discard the rest. I have a closet full of now unused humidifiers. They just did not work in my indoor growing environment because I have very high ceilings and plaster walls. No matter how long I ran those humidifiers, it was an exercise in futility. I simply could not raise the humidity above 34 percent during the dry winter months, which seem to go on forever. That being said, there are some gadgets and equipment that seem to be universally helpful no matter your environment. You will use them at the start of your journey, and you'll probably keep them in the rotation even as your experience grows.

WHAT'S IN THE BAG?

Below are some basic must-haves that will really help you succeed when you begin to build your plant collection.

- **Magnifying glass.** One thing you can't spy with your little eye are some of the plant pests when they are small and just starting to take hold. By the time you can see them with your naked eye, its already too late—you've got yourself an infestation. One of the best ways to avoid this is to regularly inspect your plants with a magnifying glass. But brace yourself, a mealybug magnified to ten times its size is pretty creepy! Now don't let me scare you. You're not going to need an exterminator. But some pests are pretty much par for the course when you have plants indoors. Mixes of simple ingredients like insecticidal soap and neem oil really do do the trick! Some pests you will want to immediately annihilate—like spider mites—others you may just shrug your shoulders at. At this point, fungus gnats are my roommates. I have tried evicting them, but it turns out they have been here long enough to claim squatters' rights.

- **A good spray bottle.** You'll need this for mixing all the concoctions you'll need for everything from cleaning the plants to managing pests to fertilizing the plants. You may even want to use a second one to mist your plants. Misting does not raise the humidity, but some people enjoy this simple act—it's time spent with your plants.

- **Soft cotton gloves.** Dust can collect on the leaves of our indoor plants. As previously mentioned, without the aid of wind and rain, you must step in and keep those leaves clean so they can soak up all that good light for photosynthesizing. A pair of cotton (or any soft fabric) gloves cuts cleaning time down in half! And it's more environmentally friendly than using piles of paper towels. You can easily wipe the tops and bottoms of leaves with your two gloved hands. The bottom of the leaf is where most creeps hide, so do not skip it even if you can't see there. You'll thank me later.

More than a few of the "must have" plant parent tools are debatable. But these? Well, I would call these essentials that will come in handy long after you've moved on from the beginner phase. Here are my essentials (clockwise from the top): magnifying glass, perlite, soil scoop, good spray bottle, scissors, moisture meter, and cotton gloves.

- **Good pair of very sharp scissors.** These are essential. There will be yellow leaves. As the plant grows, the older leaves are using a ton of energy to help develop and push out that new growth. They'll fade and yellow. When they do, simply cut them off. Our homes, no matter how many humidifiers or pebble trays we have, will never be as humid as their natural growing conditions in tropical rainforests. Sometimes you will have crispy edges. If you can't stand the look of them, simply trim away the brown edges or cut the leaf off. To do this, you'll need a nice sharp pair of scissors for a clean cut. These scissors should be for dedicated plant use only. Do not use the pair of scissors that you've tossed into the junk drawer in the kitchen and used for everything from opening envelopes to opening food packages. You need a sharp pair just for your plants.

- **Moisture meter.** Sometimes the top few inches of dry soil do not tell the whole tale, especially if you are looking at a larger potted plant. The top few inches may be dry, while the bottom inches where the roots reside are plenty moist. Next thing you know, you have yourself a case of root rot—or worse—fungus gnats! (There I go with the pests again!) A moisture meter removes the guesswork of knowing when to water, which is especially important when you first begin your plant parent journey. Just remember to remove the meter; it's not meant to sit in the plant pot.

- **Neem oil.** This liquid gold is great for managing pests and giving your plants a nice, beautiful shine without clogging their pores. A small amount mixed with a liquid castile soap goes long way. A word of warning though—it smells awful, like peanuts that have been roasted too long. But after that second or third use, you go completely nose blind to it. (I cannot say the same of your guests, so you may want to give it a day before you invite anyone over.)

- **Castile soap.** Did you know liquid dish soap isn't soap? It's actually a chemical detergent with surfactants. It's great for cutting grease on your dishes, but not so much for your plants. It can strip them of all the natural oils they need. So, stick with castile soap that has natural fatty acids that do not strip natural oils or harm your plant. It doubles as a cleaner and as a nontoxic pesticide that will not harm your plants.

- **Soil scoop.** This is a great all-purpose tool. Use it to scoop out your perlite or mix up your soil and scoop it into your planter. A simple plastic one will do, but they also have some very pretty and shiny metal scoops. (I like shiny things.)

- **Large plastic tub with lid.** Once you open those bags of soil and amendments, you'll need something airtight to store them in. The last thing you want to do is leave them open for moisture and…wait for it…pests to get in. (By now, you had to know that was coming.) Those large storage containers that are typically used for storing clothes and seasonal junk are great for organizing your soils and keeping them dry. You can store the bags inside the containers, or you can premix your soil and safely store it ready to use. In the warmer months, when I find myself repotting constantly, this is my go-to storage solution. It saves one step in the repotting process.

I enjoy misting some of my plants, especially this *Epipremnum* 'Manjula'. The way the moisture beads up on those painterly leaves is so pretty. While I enjoy this plant task, I know that it is, in effect, useless if I am trying to raise the humidity. Misting does not do that. But if it is something you enjoy doing with your plants, mist away!

No humidifier, no problem

In the beginning of this plant journey, I bought all the things that I saw other plant collectors using, including big, expensive humidifiers. I live in New York, and it is very dry in my house during the long winter months, thanks to my furnace. So, I thought I needed humidifiers. I ran and ran them, trying to give my plants an extra boost of moisture during the cold months. But much to my chagrin I was never able to get my humidity over the 34 percent mark. I live in a house that is over 100 years old with 10-foot (3 m) high ceilings and plaster walls that absorb humidity. So it was a losing battle. I'm not sure there is a humidifier in existence that is going to get the job done for me. But on the next page, I provide some ways to increase humidity for your plants without a humidifier.

- **Pebble tray.** This became my go-to fix for the winter months. A pebble tray is a tray or shallow dish filled with pebbles and water. To use it, sit the plants on top of the pebbles. You can use anything to hold the pebbles. I have found that shallow bowls, organizers, or even serving platters with high sides work great! After you choose your vessel, add pebbles and warm water. When you place the plant on the tray, make sure the drainage holes are not sitting directly on the pebbles. Add a small saucer between the planter and pebbles, or drop the plant into a decorative pot without holes to make sure the plant doesn't sit in the water. The pebble tray will not increase the humidity in the room. Rather it will increase the humidity in the air immediately surrounding the plant as the water from the pebbles evaporates. That's all the plant needs.

- **Group plants together.** Now, this is the cutest thing EVER! Plants grouped together will conspire together to create a tropical microclimate through their transpiration. When we water plants, they don't use all of that moisture. A majority of the moisture is transpired (released through the tiny stomata on their leaves). They draw the moisture up from the soil and release it out through the stomata on their leaves. While the humidity in the room doesn't change, the humidity around the plant is increased as the vapor is released around them.

- **Greenhouse cabinet.** You can convert a curio cabinet meant to house knickknacks into a greenhouse. Not only will it increase the humidity for the plants housed in the cabinet, it will create quite a beautiful display case for your plants. But be warned, there is much more involved than just plunking your plants into the cabinet. The cabinet will have to be outfitted with fans, lights, trays, and tempered glass shelves that resist shattering.

I bet you were hoping to see misting included in this list. I'm sorry to say, misting will not increase the humidity for your plant—not even temporarily. It does nothing but moisten the leaves for a short time. That being said, it also does not harm the plant and many plant parents enjoy the act of misting their plants. It gives them a chance to hang out with their plants. So, mist away if you enjoy doing it. Take note, there are some velvety-leaved plants that don't like water sitting on their leaves so misting is a no-no for them.

This pebble tray will raise the humidity around this grouping of fittonias and a begonia. The water in the tray will evaporate and the plants grouped closely together will transpire and share moisture through their leaves. While it will not increase the humidity in the room, it will create a tropical microclimate the plants will love.

CHAPTER 4

Would You Date That Plant?

The Power of Reciprocity in Human and Plant Relationships—
and the Art of Letting Go

Would you date that plant? The question may
sound a little crazy, but it is not. We are in a relationship with our plants. When you examine it
closely, that relationship is not much different
from our relationships with people. Well, maybe
just a little different, but a relationship all the
same. In the relationship, plants will teach and
remind us of valuable lessons, many of which we
can carry into our relationships with people.

This *Monstera adansonii* knows my love language is NEW GROWTH! This beauty is a constant grower and shower. It thrives in bright, indirect light and likes to dry between watering. It matches my laid-back plant parenting style. Matching energy is an important ingredient for success when collecting plants. This is true for both the plant and the plant parent. If you know you are not the type to pitch humidity tents in your living room, then velvety-leaved Anthuriums probably aren't the plants for you.

What is the most important part of a relationship? (And I mean truly the most important.) It tops romance, passion, mystery, and adventure. It's even more important than attraction. Have you guessed it yet? Oh, come on! It is reciprocity. The equal parts of give and take; the two-way street; the balance. No one wants to date a vampire—well maybe some do, but that's another book. What you put into a relationship, you also want and deserve in return.

You are probably wondering, "How can you learn about reciprocity in a relationship from a plant?" It's easy. With plants, reciprocity is tangible and can actually be seen. When you pour your love and attention into the plant, if it is the one for you, it reciprocates that love and attention and gives it back to you in the form of new growth. Nothing says *I love you* like a shiny new leaf or a flower bud. If you are giving it your all—good light, careful watering, humidity, regular cleaning—and the plant gives you nothing back, or worse, it only struggles, that may not be the plant for you. Examine the relationship closely. Believe me, there is a plant out there for you—just maybe not that one. You cannot meet its needs, and it will do nothing for your sense of confidence to grow and develop as a plant parent. That plant does not know that your love language is growth.

Now apply that to people. We've all been there. Whether it was a romantic or platonic relationship, I'm willing to bet we've all been in at least one relationship with a vampire. Someone who just drained you dry, took all that you were offering with no reciprocity. And hey, no one loves vampires more than me. They are my favorite supernatural creatures! I once asked my oldest if she was turned would she want to be turned at her current age—I think she was about ten at the time (don't judge me)—or would she want to wait until she was little older. Remember that scene with Kirsten Dunst in *Interview with the Vampire* when she kept cutting her hair? Whew, that was some performance! Well, my daughter hadn't seen the movie, but she wisely chose to wait until she was older should the opportunity arise. I am way off track here. My point is, while they're cool supernatural creatures to watch in movies and television shows, they are horrible relationship partners. You deserve reciprocity. If you are willingly giving your time, care, and attention—then you deserve those in return. If your plants can give that to you, so can that person. People only treat you the way you allow them to. If there is no reciprocity in a relationship, ask yourself, "Do I deserve more?" You know the answer is yes. Like the plant, that person may not be the person for you.

Some plants are to be loved from afar—way, way afar. This asparagus fern is such a plant. I don't know what type of "fern magic" my mom has, but I did not inherit it.

Boston ferns have such beautiful broad fronds. They are an immediate vibe when added to any décor or, if you are lucky enough to live in their hardiness zone, any yard. They are the plant of my childhood memories, and I desperately wanted to grow them, too.

Love the One That Loves You Back!

Plants will teach you the value of reciprocity and when it's time to let it go. Take my relationship with *Nephrolepis exaltata* 'Bostoniensis', commonly known as the Boston fern. It also bears the nickname sword fern, which makes sense since it stabbed me right in the heart. My relationship with Boston ferns was toxic. I mean really, really toxic. I loved them so, but they simply did not love me back. And believe me, I kept trying even though it was pretty clear in its messaging. Sometimes the one that ain't for us lets us know that loudly and clearly. We just don't receive the message.

I never met a Boston fern that I didn't bring right home and try to grow. I ignored the past lessons and kept repeating my same mistakes. I wanted to make that fern bend to my stubborn will, even as the fronds dropped with each passing minute. No matter what I did—mist it hourly, place it right next to the humidifier (this was in another house with lower ceilings)—it still didn't work. I moved it to the bathroom, let it take showers with me, sleep on my side of the bed, borrow my husband's slippers—no matter what I did, the plant always died. But not without letting me know just how incredibly unhappy it was in my care. Within hours of bringing it home the plant would begin to yellow and get crispy. (Okay, so maybe it was not hours, but it happened FAST.) And each time one died, I experienced a fresh new heartache. I would pour my feelings into my journal and vow to never love a Boston fern again. But of course, that wasn't true. They had a hold on me. What was I to do? The heart wants what it wants. You know how there are some songs that are like the soundtrack to your life at different points? Well, I had plants.

Boston ferns were in the corner of my most fond (I was going to say frond, but I resisted—for that I deserve a new plant) childhood memories. If I sit quietly and concentrate, I can conjure up the smells of the apartment from my childhood.

It smelled like a loamy forest just after a spring rain. My mom had big fluffy ferns hanging in front of just about every window. In one corner sat a rain lamp that I was fairly obsessed with. Rain lamps are vintage gold now; they were kitsch then, but I loved ours. My mom's lamp was brass, with a woman standing in a bed of ferns. There were strings all along the outside of the lamp and mineral oil "rained" down the strings. Man, I wish I had that lamp today! The lamp sat on a table, and my mom circled the base of the table with dainty asparagus ferns. I was wise enough to know not to even look their way. I didn't want it with them. But I wanted the Boston ferns, and I would not be denied. You're probably saying, "Stop buying Boston ferns." That would make the most sense, but let's not pretend we always make the best decisions when we are in a relationship, desperately trying to make it work. I kept buying them, expecting a long-term commitment. But they were not here for it. I was met with heartache and crispy, withered fronds. I needed to move on. The question is, did I? Keep reading.

It's Not You, It's Your Environment

Finally, I stopped and examined my relationship with Boston ferns. It was not a healthy one. All I did was give, give, and give. All they did was take and gave me literally nothing in return. Not even one new frond to watch unfurl. Have you ever seen a fern frond unfurl? (Trying saying that fast ten times in a row!) It is very cool, and I wanted that. You know the saying, "Everything ain't for everybody?" The same is true of plants, and I had to learn that. Boston ferns were not for me—there was no reciprocity.

So instead, I dated other ferns. Very casually at first, I didn't want to get my heart broken again. I moved slowly, to see if I could find one to match my energy and enthusiasm. I quickly learned it should not be the maidenhair. That one was so very beautiful but spiteful and mean for no reason at all.

While it took some time to learn that Boston ferns were not for me, this maidenhair fern taught me quickly, and with razor sharp precision, that it was not the one for my very dry house. It did not come to play with me. Those beautiful delicate fronds would never be a part of my collection.

I'm telling you, it died much faster than any Boston fern that I'd ever met and in the most dramatic manner. The Boston fern at least had the decency to leave behind a few fronds, just for sentimental sake. Like, to remind me of what we once had, no matter how short-lived. That maidenhair fern would shrivel to nothing, like it had never even been there. It left no trace, just an empty pot. Well, there was still the soil, so I guess it wasn't totally empty. But not a trace of a frond.

No matter how much I tried, the maidenhair fern would not bend to my will. It is so delicate and beautiful it was hard for me to resist at first, but I finally did. Those dainty black stems hold little to no water, meaning this beauty needed to be watered almost every day. This fern did not match my laid-back plant parenting style any more than the Boston fern did—it was not the one for me. It was hurtful and almost made me swear off ferns altogether. I was almost ready to put them all behind me; it was simply not meant to be. Almost.

Just when I thought all was lost, I stumbled upon the Crispy Wave—a fern so different from all of the others. Instead of small delicate leafy fronds, it has these big paddle-like fronds that feel like lettuce and kind of look like a Boston fern leaflet. Kind of. Which reminds me of a funny story about the first time I bought one. You're going to think I'm making this up, but I promise this is the nothing but the truth, the whole truth, so help me fern god.

So, I'm in the supermarket—they are basically plant shops now. Let me be clear, that is not a complaint. Quite the opposite, I love it! It saves me a stop on my errands run, but if I don't go in with a list, I'll come out with several plants and none of what I went in there for. Even with a list, sometimes my bags have more plants than groceries. So, as I'm checking a tomato for ripeness, I look up and see the most beautiful plant specimen. Okay, so that's not entirely true. I pushed my cart right past the produce section and stopped at the plants first. I have my priorities in order.

When I picked it up, I knew there was no way I could leave that store without that plant. After ringing some of my groceries, the cashier gets to the plant. She picks it up and starts turning it around in her hands. Finally, she looks at me and asks, "What kind of lettuce is this?" When I tell you I howled, I mean I howled. And it was one of those throw your head back surprised laughs, the really loud kind. She thought it was only mildly funny when I told her it was a plant. She was annoyed by my raucous laughter, so I didn't bother to explain that I thought it looked like lettuce too and seriously wanted to take a bite. I never knew ferns could look like that! I started with the Crispy Wave and have since also added a crocodile fern—also found at a grocery store.

Crispy Wave taught me that it wasn't me, it was my environment that was wrecking my fern relationships. Not every fern is created equal.

It's a love connection! The *Asplenium nidus* cultivar, commonly known as the Crispy Wave fern, matched my energy and enthusiasm. And more importantly, it matched my growing environment without a hitch! Unlike the others, this fern was able to adapt to average household humidity and a chill plant parent style.

I had to kiss quite a few frogs—and kill a few plants—before I finally found the fern for me! Unlike the other ferns, the Crispy Wave matches my enthusiasm and laid-back plant parenting style. The Boston fern simply needed more humidity than I could ever give it in my house in New York. My ceilings were too high. No humidifier was going to raise the humidity in my rooms to 80 percent (not without causing serious household problems), and my winters with indoor heat are too dry. While my mom had much success with Boston ferns, her growing environment was strikingly different from mine. Namely, her ceilings were much lower. It was much easier to give the ferns the humidity they craved. With that Boston fern, I could have popped a humidity tent up in my living room to meet its needs, but it would have been a bridge too far just to make that plant happy. I don't want a tent in my living room. If you are going beyond what you are comfortable with in a relationship—whether with a plant or person—it's definitely time to end that relationship. Unlike the other ferns, the Crispy Wave was able to acclimate to average household humidity and my relaxed plant parenting style. It was a love connection!

The Crispy Wave showed me the meaning of true fern love. And now here we are—I water, she grows. It's a beautiful thing! The moral of the story is . . . *Every plant ain't for everybody.* And that's okay. There is a saying that goes, "There is a lid for every pot." And as it turns out, there is a plant for every plant parent. You just have to find the one that works for you in your home. No matter how many times you fail, just remember— that plant is out there.

HAPPY PLANTS, HAPPY YOU

The Art of Letting Go

Sometimes it is time to let go. Plants will teach you this too. When you let go of something that no longer serves you, you make room for new growth. Whether it is a yellowed leaf or a toxic friend, if it makes you feel badly or doubt yourself, let it go. You cannot fix that yellowed leaf, I promise you this. No amount of watering or adjustments in light or fertilizer is going to turn that leaf green again. Its time has come; just cut it off and move on. Notice how much happier the plant looks without that yellowed leaf? Do you also notice the relief you feel when you look at the plant and that yellowed leaf is gone? That is how it goes when you remove something from your life that has served its purpose.

A yellow leaf is not necessarily a sign of something being wrong with the plant or your plant-care routine. It is often a sign that the leaf has run its course. It has contributed all the energy that it has to give to the plant. Look closely, and you will see that a new leaf has emerged on the plant, replacing that old spent leaf. The plant has grown, and the new leaf is even bigger and prettier than the one that has withered. This is the natural cycle of a plant, just as sometimes it is the natural cycle of a relationship.

Thank the leaf for the lessons it taught you—how much watering the plant needs, the proper lighting, and frequency of fertilizer. The plant will teach you that it is okay to cut that leaf off and move on. That relationship has lessons to teach you too. Every relationship that ends is not a failed relationship, it's a lesson. What have you learned about yourself? What are your needs, and what are your wants? There are some things in a relationship that are negotiable while other things are dealbreakers. When a relationship ends, take inventory of those negotiables and dealbreakers. Carry this new knowledge about yourself into the next relationship. My plants have taught me that I am not about that very high-maintenance plant life. My plants are a point of peace and relaxation. That translates into low maintenance.

While there are plenty of tips for diagnosing and troubleshooting a problem when your plant is struggling to try and save it, don't forget the other lesson that your plants are trying to teach you—the art of letting go. When a plant is on the decline, it is okay to get rid of it. Letting it go may mean giving it to someone else to rehab or adding it to the compost bin. I struggled with this at the beginning of my plant journey. I wanted to save them all! At one point, I had more plants in rehab than plants living their best life. The more they would struggle, so would I as a plant parent. Seeing those yellowed leaves undermined my confidence in growing and made me second guess everything I was doing with the other plants that were not on the struggle bus. I thought about getting rid of them, but then I would feel tremendous guilt. And you know what I've already said about that emotion—it is totally useless. This push-pull was also robbing me of the reason I started collecting plants in the first place—enjoyment.

With each dying plant, enjoyment dwindled. What had been leisurely was turning burdensome. I had to refocus and remind myself why I had started on this journey. If keeping plants on the struggle bus was taking me off of that path, I needed to let those struggling plants go. I pushed past the little pangs of guilt and got rid of the struggling plants. The ones that still had plenty of life in them, I passed on to friends and family. The others went on to meet their maker in the great garden beyond. You know what I felt? Relief. Those plants had not been not well suited to my indoor growing environment. I had to learn to accept that and move on. Plants are your path to peace, not to more obligation and burden.

A yellow leaf is not always a sign of a problem. It is natural for the older, lower leaves of a plant to yellow after they have contributed all that energy to the plant's new growth. It's time to cut this older yellowed leaf on my *Philodendron burle-marxii*.

Yellow leaf? Do not panic!

A yellow leaf is not always a sign of a problem. As the plant grows, the lower, older leaves will yellow and drop off. It takes a lot of energy to photosynthesize, produce oxygen, and push out lush new growth. And if the plant also flowers—well, forget about it! There will be yellowing leaves. This is just a part of its natural life cycle. A good indication that it's just the life cycle of the plant and there's nothing wrong systemically is when the yellowing leaves are the lower, older leaves, and the plant appears otherwise healthy. Of course, there are times when you should check for something more. If the leaves are yellowing all over the plant:

Sometimes you have to check out the roots to diagnose the plant. This *Aglaonema* 'Red Valentine' was still in its original nursery pot. While the roots were healthy, it was way overpotted and needed to go down in planter size. The root system was small. The plant did not need that much soil.

Check the plant for pests

Some pests are bothersome—I'm looking at you fungus gnats. Others, like the dreaded spider mites and scale, will damage your plants by literally sucking the life out of them. Get all up in your plant's business with a magnifying glass or jeweler's loupe. Thoroughly inspect all the leaves. Dig around and inspect the soil too. If no pests are detected, but the problem persists, move to the next step.

Check the roots

Option 1
If the leaves are yellowing and the plant looks droopy, check the soil and roots. If the soil has been soggy for a prolonged time, there may be root rot. Pop the plant out of the planter and check the roots. Rotting roots turn dark and mushy. If this is the case, cut away the bad roots and salvage any healthy roots. Repot it into fresh soil, and water sparingly until there are signs of recovery.

Option 2
If the roots are light colored and not mushy but there are more roots than soil in the pot, then the plant is having a hard time holding onto moisture. It's time for a repot. Increase the planter size—but no more than 1 or 2 inches (2.5 or 5 cm) wider—and give the plant fresh soil.

Option 3
If the roots look healthy and white, with plenty of soil around them, proceed to the next step.

Check for thirst

Now what I say next may sound like I'm trying to trick you, but I promise I'm not. While a yellowing, droopy plant can be a sign the plant is overwatered, it can also be a sign of thirst. I know, I know. It would be a lot easier if the symptoms did not overlap, but they do and here we are. Once again, pop your plant out of the planter. Is the soil bone dry or mostly dry and you recently watered your plant? Then your soil has become hydrophobic. Hydrophobic soil is soil that stops absorbing water. When this happens water will just run down the sides of the pot and right out of the drainage holes without soaking into the soil. If this is the case, repot the plant and give it fresh new soil. If it is dry and you haven't watered it in a while, well that is the easiest fix of all—just water the plant.

Less Is More

Now this is the real kicker, the real punch to the gut—sometimes we do too much. That can be really hard to hear. Especially when you think all that you are doing is beneficial. No amount of watering and fawning is going to make a plant grow faster. Sometimes it is overkill—literally. Too much water, too much sun, too much repotting, too much attention. Plants are going to do what they do, at their own pace, no matter the effort we put in. Do your best to provide the best conditions in your home, and slowly back away from the plant.

We cannot control everything. I want all of my hoyas to bloom; instead, only a few have bloomed. All I can do is provide them with the light and water that they need. They rest is going to be up to them. Plants will teach you to redirect that energy to the things that are within your control. And that list is short. In fact, there's only one thing on it—you. The real lesson is: That's okay. We can't control whether someone will like us or think we're smart enough or pretty enough or qualified enough. But we can control how we react and how much stock we put into their opinions—and that's all it is, an opinion. Need I remind you what they say about opinions? Everyone's got one.

This tiny bloom on my *Hoya bilobata* was such a happy surprise. When I added hoyas to my collection it was for their beautiful waxy foliage. I had no idea how smitten I would be with their otherworldly blooms.

HAPPY PLANTS, HAPPY YOU

Can I get a hoya bloom?

I'm sure on this journey you will add a few hoyas to your collection. You'll probably follow the path of many before you: You will fall in love with their foliage, and then you will obsess over getting them to bloom. When I first began collecting these beauties, everything I read said the plant had to be quite mature before there was any chance of seeing a bloom. Well, that proved to be not quite so accurate. None of the hoyas in my collection are more than three years old, and many have bloomed for me, even a *Hoya macrophylla* after it graduated to a plant from the one-leaf rooted cutting club. Age did not seem to matter. I'll tell you what did. I gave it an extended period of drought and loads of very bright light. As the cold winter months came to an end and the weather began to warm up, I allowed my semi-succulent hoyas to thoroughly dry over a period of four to five weeks. My hoyas live in a very bright area of my house that gets hours of direct, bright light. At the end of that period, I resumed watering with a diluted liquid fertilizer and BAM! I was rewarded with an embarrassment of peduncle riches! In one year, over half of my hoyas bloomed. It was thrilling! My *H. callisto-phylla* had eight blooms all at once. That level of excitement almost took me out! When I tell you, I carried on so bad when I made the discovery. My family was very sick of me that day, but Jimmy crack corn and I don't care! I would do it all again, should that plant again bless me with that many blooms all at once. So, if it's blooms you want, a dry spell and lots of light for your semi-succulent hoyas may just do the trick.

I was doing the absolute most in my busyness. But it turns out, while I thought it was all good, it was wearing me all the way out. I was giving it all away, leaving my well bone dry. When I would bristle at the question, "What do you do?" it was because I foolishly cared too much about what I thought others would think of what I did. I don't even know what they thought. I never once answered the dreaded question and followed it up with, "What do you think of that?" Instead, I created this entire fantasy of what I imagined they thought of what I was doing, and, as a fix, I did the absolute most. I nearly burned myself out in my quest to escape judgment from others. And the truth of it is, no matter what I was doing they might have found something to judge. People can be judgy. Like super judgy. At the end of the day, their judgment or what they thought did not matter. When I fell in love with caring for plants, it was such a point of joy and peace, there was no way I was going to let anyone else's opinions sully that. What other people think of you is beyond your control, and frankly it's none of your business. At first, it can be scary to just let go of caring about other's opinions, but ultimately it is freeing. Pour your energy into being the best YOU you can be. Letting go of what others may think of you is an act of self-love. What do you think of you? Your opinion of you is the only one that matters. Make sure it's a good one.

CHAPTER 5

A Date with Yourself

Learn How to Pause with Plants.
Time Spent with Your Plants is Time Spent with Yourself

The journey to self-care starts with a date. Not a date with someone else, but a date with yourself. We've all been on been on a date or two, or had a night out with friends, at some point in our lives. We set aside some time, planned an activity—dinner or a movie, maybe both—got dressed up and put on our favorite scent. But when was the last time you did these things just for yourself? When was the last time you carved out some time to enjoy your own company without the added company of someone else? Because that time with others can go both ways. Sometimes it is great, and a good time is had by all. But then there are those times when you spend the whole time worrying if the other person is having a good time, or worse, you keep sneaking glances at the time to see when you can get the hell out of there. A date with yourself removes those variables and is pure pleasure.

And I get it, sometimes hanging out alone can be intimidating because we jumble up being alone with being lonely. You can feel lonely as hell in a room full of people. Being alone does not mean you are lonely. The two are not the same thing. That's where plants come in. If you don't have any, plants can help clear a path to spending quality time with yourself. They offer an opportunity to hang out with just yourself in a way that is meaningful and relaxing. It's almost something that I had forgotten how to do. So much of my life was filled with other people.

Whether you are an introvert or an extrovert, I am a firm believer in the benefits of spending some time alone with yourself to relax, refresh, and recharge. And not just time alone, but unplugged, nontech time alone. The world we live in is so driven by technology that tech masks itself as a connection. But it is not a true connection. To really connect, you must sometimes disconnect. When you pause with plants, it is a chance to unplug and recharge yourself and your spirit. I love plant shopping, obviously. But really, I just love being surrounded by plants, quiet in my thoughts. It makes me feel connected to nature.

Before beginning this plant journey, I did not connect with nature nearly enough as an adult. Sure, during the warmer months I would spend time outdoors in nature, but I live in the northeastern region of the US. We have more cold than warm months, and it can get really, really cold. When those temps drop—and I'm talking dropping below freezing into the twenties and teens, even—I retreat indoors. I am not about that "outdoors in the cold" life. That means I'm left with only a few months of the year to frolic outside and get my hands in the dirt.

Being surrounded by plants presents an opportunity to unplug and spend time with yourself. And, frankly, plants make me feel like a goddess. I don't need much more of a reason than that to spend time caring for them.

Reconnecting with indoor plants has expanded my time with nature from a few months out of the year to year-round. Whether I am connecting in my home or taking really long trips to the nursery, or better, visiting botanical gardens, I am spending much more time with these green beings than I ever did before, and the results are magical. Spending time in nature, including with indoor plants, can help reduce anxiety, stress, and sharpen your focus. Getting our hands in some dirt has been scientifically proven to boost serotonin levels. Soil contains good bacteria—*Mycobacterium vaccae*—that triggers our brain to release serotonin. Bringing plants into your home not only adds beauty to your surroundings, but it is also believed to improve your overall health.

Just Add Music and Candles

When you spend time with your plants, make it a date! When I first started my plant parent journey, I watered my fiddle-leaf fig without any fanfare. It was just one of the day's tasks. And then that plant started to thrive, and I started paying more attention to my routine and, of course, added more plants. As my collection grew, watering my plants began to take longer. And as my collection grew, I began to connect more with my plants and myself. Watering day started to take on a life all its own. It was not a task, but rather something that I very much looked forward to. I carved out time to do it and protected that time in my schedule. When it was time to water my plants, other invites did not stand a chance.

Adding candles and music turns what could be a mundane task into a relaxing self-care ritual.

My plant-care routine evolved into a self-care routine as I created an entire ritual surrounding getting my plants watered.

At first it was just a small thing—lighting a few candles and some incense. Potted plants make great incense holders by the way. Most of the time I watered plants when I had the house to myself, so I cranked up my favorite tunes. I don't know when it happened, but I also started getting dressed up. Well, sort of. There was an account I followed on TikTok, and the woman designed elaborate dressing gowns—not to be confused with a robe. They were straight out of old Hollywood. I ordered one with the idea that I'd take it on our next fancy trip. And then COVID-19 hit, and there were no fancy trips, but I still had that robe (I mean dressing gown) in my closet. At some point I started wearing it to water my plants. I think it started the day I was horsing around in it, making it billow out behind me like Darth Vader's cape. It was the perfect thing to wear while I floated around the house checking on my green babies. Music, candles, and a fancy robe (over my pajamas or sweats) turned what could have been a mundane task into a very intentional self-care ritual involving all of the senses. It's a date with myself.

When you're hanging with your plants, take it up level and turn it into an intentional ritual. Make a playlist of your favorite songs, add candles or incense and a ridiculously fancy outfit, and voila, it's a vibe! The quality time you spend with your plants is quality time you spend with yourself. When I am watering my plants and checking on them, I am literally doing the same thing for myself. When you are caring for plants, you can make it a dance party or an ambulatory mediation or just a daydream. Why do adults stop daydreaming? Let's get back to that.

Connect with Nature

Most times when you hear this expression, you think of being in the great outdoors. Sure, that is one way to connect with nature. But growing and caring for houseplants is also a means of connecting with nature. It is a true connectedness. While caring for these green beings, we develop a strong bond and relationship. This bonding with nature not only makes us all kinds of happy, but it can also spark creativity and calmness. Keeping up with the names and different care requirements of your plants also helps sharpen your focus and boost your memory. I even surprise myself when I can remember and identify so many different plants. It's like my memory sharpens with each new plant that joins the family.

Get Your Hands Dirty!

Repotting is probably at the top of the list of favorite things to do with my plants. So little Suzy has been growing for a while, and you want to upgrade her pot? There are a few things to keep in mind before getting your hands dirty. When it comes to planters, size matters! As a rule, only go up one or two inches (2.5 or 5 cm) wider in pot size. A quick way to see if the size is right: Drop the old pot into the intended new pot to see how much more room your plant will have. Generally, you don't want to add depth, just a little room to the circumference. There should be only an inch or two of space between the two pots.

Why is the size so important? A pot that is too big means more soil that can stay wet for prolonged periods, and that can lead to root rot.

This *Dracaena masoniana*, commonly known as the whale fin snake plant, is due for a repot. But the pot I wanted to use is too big. Overpotting is a common mistake. To find the right size, just drop the current pot into the intended new pot to make sure there isn't too much room.

111

Soil that remains damp can also lead to—you guessed it—those dreaded fungus gnats! A pot that is sized just right means the plant roots will be able to quickly access and use up the moisture in the soil so that it does not remain damp. Resist the urge to buy that huge pot so that the plant will have room to grow. This is a common mistake. When you repot, you'll probably be shocked how small the plant's root system is compared to all of the action up top with the plant's stems and leaves.

How often should you repot? Well for this one there really is no right answer. It is believed that most plants prefer a snug fit around their roots and not being smothered in too much soil. They want their roots to feel all tucked in and cozy. Some plant families are epiphytic in nature—that means that in the wild, they grow up in the trees, secured to the bark. They don't grow in soil. So, when we grow them indoors, a smaller pot with less soil is the way to go.

What about new plants when you first bring them home? This is probably one of the most hotly debated topics within the plant community. I'm going to settle the debate right here and right now—it depends. Not the answer you were looking for, right? But there really is no one correct answer. Repot immediately or wait? Both answers are the right answer, depending upon your plant parenting style.

For me, I like to wait and allow the plant time to acclimate to its new home. My indoor growing conditions are going to be markedly different from the greenhouse or nursery where it spent the first part of its life. My guess is, there will probably be a little less light and way less humidity here in my home. Like way, way less. In the winter, my house is straight up arid. The plant must get used to that before I go snatching it out of the soil that it has been successfully growing and thriving in. I don't want to shock it more than I have to. After it has been with me for a few months and is still growing and thriving, I know that it can live in this new environment. Only then do I consider repotting it. I know it can survive here. This is my general rule. Unless of course I spot a problem like pests or really low-quality soil. Then that wait period goes right out the window and I repot immediately. And now we're back at square one with my original answer—it all depends. You'll find this to be the answer in most scenarios involving plants. There is no one-size-fits-all.

Look at these juicy roots and rhizomes! These ZZ plants do not need to be repotted often, but these two are ready to go up a planter size. They were in 4-inch (10 cm) pots. I am moving them up just 2 inches (5 cm), to 6-inch (15 cm) planters.

When it's time to repot, gather up your tools before getting started. Here are my repotting essentials: soil scoop, chunky soil already mixed up and ready to go, a little window screen over the drainage hole to keep the soil in the pot when you water, new pot, mini spade and clippers to trim unhealthy leaves, and, of course, the plant you are repotting.

Material matters

In addition to picking the right size, the material the planter is made of matters too.

Terra cotta. Because of their porousness, clay pots are great for drought-loving plants like succulents and cacti. This planter material is not well suited for plants that like to remain consistently moist, like calatheas and ferns. Always give your clay planter a good soaking prior to use. This will help it not dry out as quickly when in use. If you use clay pots for plants other than succulents and cacti, be prepared to water a little more often.

Ceramic. This material is not porous and will hold onto moisture longer than clay pots. Of course, I recommend that if you are planting directly into a ceramic pot, make sure it has a drainage hole.

Plastic nursery pots. This is also a nonporous material and will hold onto moisture longer. Plastic nursery pots are great because they generally have many more drainage holes than both terra cotta and ceramic pots. They can be dropped into decorative pots for a prettier look. I like to switch up my plant's looks often, so most of my plants are planted directly in plastic pots and dropped into pretty, decorative pots for display.

Terra cotta pots are a great option for plants that like to stay on the dry side. They are also great if you are a little heavy-handed when it comes to watering. Its porous nature means clay does not retain moisture for long.

Succulents need drought and are well suited for terra cotta planters.

When a Hole Is Not Enough

On this plant journey, you will often hear the phrase "well-draining soil." But what does this mean? It means soil that is not compacted and has great airflow for the plant roots. It is soil that both releases excess water and also provides adequate moisture. Well-draining soil is not usually what you will find in a bag of all-purpose potting soil. You will need to amend it with something. It sounds like magic, but you won't need any spell to get well-draining soil. It's fairly simple to achieve by amending that bag of general potting soil with a few things.

- **Perlite or pumice.** These are the most basic and magical of ingredients. Both help aerate the soil, help get moisture to the roots, and help nutrients from fertilizers release more slowly. If you add nothing else, add perlite. Pumice is a little more environmentally friendly and provides the same benefits. However, it is not always available in large quantities.

- **Orchid bark.** The name can be a little confusing, because it is not actually bark from an orchid but rather the medium that orchids are typically grown in. This additive is usually a mix of pine and fir bark and sometimes has coconut husk chips. It adds even more aeration for good oxygen flow to the roots and provides nutrients. This chunky additive is great for epiphytic plants—plants that grow on trees in the wild. All of my hoyas are in super chunky soil mixes with plenty of orchid bark added in.

- **Horticultural charcoal.** A little of this goes a long way. While I'm pretty loosey-goosey with the perlite and the bark, when it comes to horticultural charcoal, I follow the recommended ratio of 10:1. Horticultural charcoal is very porous so it boosts aeration and drainage.

It also protects against fungus and harmful bacteria. These qualities can help prolong the life of the potting soil. And charcoal is great for plants that like to be consistently moist.

I don't have a precise soil mixture recipe. I let the ancestors guide me. I add the perlite and bark until they say stop (same with seasonings when I'm cooking). The ratios can be adjusted for the different types of plant. For example, for hoyas, I add extra bark for a very chunky mix. Most of the hoyas we grow in our homes are epiphytic by nature and do not grow in soil. The more air and room their roots have to move around, the better. For moisture-loving plants like ferns and calatheas, I add extra charcoal since they like their soil consistently moist. The charcoal will help prevent the growth of fungus and harmful bacteria in the moist soil.

How chunky is it? Soooo chunky! Many plants, like hoyas, monsteras, and philodendron, really thrive in a chunky, well-draining soil mix. When I am mixing soil for them, I add lots of bark, which creates pockets of air for supreme oxygen flow and drainage.

Clockwise from top: Horticultural charcoal, orchid bark, and perlite. These are my go-to additives for creating a nice, chunky, well-draining soil for my plants. With these three added ingredients, you can get just the right soil mix for every plant's needs.

Time for a Refresh

Say you know the plant is not ready for re-potting, but you want to refresh the soil a bit. You can top it off with some fresh soil, and then aerate it to help the soils mix in the pot. This will give the soil a boost of fresh nutrients. Just want a different look? Well, that is super easy! That is what those planters without holes are for. Being a bit of a commitment-phobe when it comes to choosing a look for my plants, I keep many in nursery pots. I almost never plant my plants directly in the decorative pot because, at some point, I'm going to change my mind about that plant and planter combo. So, the plastic nursery pot dropped into the decorative pot or, if you want to get fancy, a cachepot, is the way to go. The looks are endless. Just remember to take the plastic pot out for watering if the decorative pot does not have a drainage hole. Although, now there needs to be a word of warning here: If you go the drop-in route, you will probably start collecting many pretty, empty planters. Then you'll need plants to fill those empty pots. It's a never-ending cycle.

Ambulatory meditation

Have you ever tried to meditate but simply could not quiet your mind while sitting still? Here's the fix—ambulatory meditation. You can do this while checking on your plants. Ambulatory meditation is just what it sounds like. It's the act of meditating while you walk around. It might sound counter-intuitive to pair meditation and walking, but you can quiet your mind and connect with peace while walking. It is a matter of being intentional and connected to our senses, our surroundings, and the present moment. Usually when we walk, we are on autopilot. When you are practicing ambu-latory meditation, you are intentionally choosing the path you will walk, even the foot you will begin your walk with. It is intentional and focused.

Choose the group of plants you will visit when practicing ambulatory meditation. I usually use my hoyas and then move on to the large group of plants in my dining room. Slowly and systemati-cally, I go from plant to plant, touching each one deliberately and purposefully. I use the plants as a point to focus on and quiet my mind. When distracting thoughts try to enter your mind, use the plants to help refocus and clear the thoughts. Pick one up, focus on the weight of it, how it feels in your hands. Focus on the details of the leaves. This allows you to be fully present in the moment, to connect with your mind, your body, and your senses. You can take this practice further and add breathing exercises or an affir-mative mantra that you repeat with each stroke of a leaf. I have tried many times to meditate, thinking there was only one way to do it; that's to sit still and quietly in a room. No matter what, my mind would wander to the grocery list or the week's errands. Instead of connecting with my body, I felt restless and wanted to change posi-tions just about every thirty seconds. Using my plants as a device to help me focus was a happy accident. I now meditate weekly. Our thoughts are powerful, meditating with my plants has helped me be mindful and more in control of the thoughts floating in my headspace.

If your thoughts start to wander to next week's errands, grab a plant and focus on a leaf to help re-center your thoughts. I like to use variegated plants like this *Hoya carnosa* 'Rubra', the Krimson Princess hoya. My thoughts get lost in those colors, rather than in the grocery list.

Hoyas are for sure my favorite plant genus. Their waxy foliage is so interesting and unlike any of my other plants. I frequently use this grouping of hoyas as my focal point when I am practicing ambulatory meditation.

Shop for Plants Like a Pro

If you follow plant lovers online, you probably have an ever-growing and never-ending list of must-have plants. When I began my plant journey, this was me. Every time I would open my phone, I'd see a new plant that I never knew existed, and I would add it to the list. Just when I thought I was finished, bam! The 'gram would hit me with something new. Of course, I'd have to hit the nursery or plant shop (online or in person) to try and find it. Couldn't find it? No problem, I'd still get a new plant. The more plant-filled spaces I saw, the more I tried to fill my space with plants. The temporary euphoria from buying new plants was hard to resist, so I'd just get that other plant over there instead.

At first, all of my plant purchases were impulse buys, with little to no planning. It was easy to get caught up chasing the next plant. It was a vicious cycle of running out of space, and then that space would free up when that impulse buy did not make it. I quickly learned my compulsive plant shopping was not sustainable. I also learned that collecting plants is not a race to have the most plants. A collection of plants does not need to be hundreds of plants. You can have a collection of just ten plants; it is still a collection.

What matters is the quality of the plants, not the quantity. Who cares if you have hundreds of plants if they're all on the struggle bus? There were times when my collection was bursting at the seams, and it was overwhelming. Not only could I not keep up with everyone's needs, but my family was also sick of me. The plants were taking over. Every inch of kitchen counter space was covered with plants or plant paraphernalia. Folks had to learn the hard way, that was not iced tea in that jug. And before you could wash a dish, you first had to take the plants out of the sink. Same with the shower. The faucets belonged to the plants. I had to stop and take inventory and reassess. I did not stop shopping for plants. Let's not get crazy. But I stopped making impulse buys. Instead, I became more intentional in my shopping. I had to learn to shop like a pro. I could not base my purchases on looks alone. This is where I learned some real plant knowledge, and I learned how to shop like a pro.

- **Go down the research rabbit hole.** When you are hit with a plant you've never seen before but must have it, go on and add it to your wish list. But leave it right there until you've done at least a cursory search of the plant's needs first. Some of the prettiest plants I discovered were also the neediest. They did not stand a chance in this dry house, but I hadn't bothered to do the research first. I could have saved us both some heartache. Now I research a little first. Do you have what it takes to give the plant what it needs? Is your light right? What about humidity? If your answer is no, save yourself some heartache and just love that plant from afar.

- **Start looking weird.** Do you have what your plant needs? If your answer is yes, move onto the next step and go get the plant. But how do you choose which one, when there are dozens of great-looking specimens of the plant. Here's where it gets fun. You're going to have to get comfortable looking weird real fast.

- **Check the new leaf size.** It's hard to really see which plant is lush and giving botanical baddie when they're all clumped together. Select at least three, remove them from the shelf and line them up on the floor, or in your cart—just a spot that has room to really examine them. Now you want to look at the size of the leaves, especially any new ones pushing their way out. If the plant is very newly propagated, the new growth will be tiny and much smaller than the large, mother leaves you see lower on the plant. There's nothing wrong with that, but knowing this helps you manage your expectations about what the plant will look like as it grows. Ideally, look for plants with nice sized leaves and juicy sized new growth. That usually indicates the plant is well established and mature.

- **Look for pests.** So you've narrowed it down, and you're ready to make your pick. Hold on! Take a really good look around for pests. Yup, pests. The plants have been living amongst each other and maybe have shared more than a little transpired moisture. I once visited a very posh plant boutique not too far from me. They had a beautiful collection of calatheas— I know, I know. But they are so pretty, and I am weak. Luckily for me on this day, said calatheas were covered in mealybugs. It was divine intervention. It doesn't matter where you shop, inspect those plants.

- **Count plants per pot.** Okay so now you have (at least) three plants that have passed the sniff test, but you still can't decide which one to get. I would be remiss if I didn't remind you that you can get all three. Too far? Okay, fine, you want to narrow it down to one. Just standing there staring at the plants is not going to help you choose which one to buy. Instead, use the PPP formula to choose the very best specimen: That's the formula of plants per pot. Pick each plant up and count the number of stems you see in the pot. The one with the most is the one you get. That's the most bang for your buck. When you get them home, you can leave them in the pot together as they were sold or divide them up. Sometimes there are as many as three plants in one pot. I love to sprinkle plants everywhere, so I often opt to divide them and spread the plant love around the house. Other times, that lush full plant is too beautiful to bother.

This plant-filled aisle at Larchmont Nurseries is as close to paradise as I can get without getting on an airplane. When I am shopping for plants, this is my first stop. Choosing just one plant to bring home is a struggle!

So you have a new plant?
Don't let it play with the others!

When you bring new plants home, do not immediately introduce them to your other plants. You should inspect them for pests with a magnifying glass. Even if you do not spot any, assume there are plenty teeming below in the soil of the plant and quarantine it nonetheless for at least two weeks before introducing it to the rest of your collection. No matter where you buy your plants—whether it is from a posh plant shop or a big box store—there is always the chance that there are a few uninvited guests in the soil or hiding beneath a leaf. It's just par for the course. After inspecting and quarantining, you can also give the plant a good spray down with a mix of insecticidal soap and water.

If there are pests, it does not mean that the place you bought them from does not take care of their plants, and it certainly does not mean that you are a bad plant parent. The soil our plants grows in is teeming with all manner of life (mostly good but sometimes harmful), much of which we cannot see. It is practically impossible to have pest-free plants. On one of my frequent trips to the botanical garden, I noticed a beautiful enormous bird of paradise plant literally covered in mealybugs. I did not see any SWAT teams racing over in hazmat suits to hose and

spray the plant down. It is just part of nature and the circle of life. While I'm sure you won't want that to be the case in your home, there is no need for panic if you spot a few unwanted friends. What you want to do is prevent their spread by keeping new plants in their own area until you feel it's safe for them to play with the others. The quarantine area can be in a separate room, or the same room in a plastic tub far removed from the others. Some plant pests are just bothersome—like fungus gnats—others are a menace and can take out your collection. So do not skimp on that quarantine period.

If you spot pests, you have a choice to make. Either you keep the plant and try to treat it to get rid of the pests, or you get rid of the plant. I once ordered a *Goeppertia (Calathea) warszewiczii*. It arrived with a few friends in tow—spider mites! And it wasn't just a few, it was a full webby infestation. They probably thought it was party time when they were in that dark and quiet box on their way to me. I thought about trying to treat and quarantine the plant because I was really smitten with that velvety leaf. But ultimately, I decided it was in my and the rest of my collection's best interests to get a refund and toss the plant instead.

These new additions to the plant family are in quarantine on a shelf in the hallway until it's safe for them to play with the others. Pick a spot away from your other plants for your new entries. You do not want to immediately introduce them to the rest of the plant gang until you know they do not have any pest stowaways.

CHAPTER 6

Gratuitous Beauty

Finding the Best Houseplants for Your Space
and Appreciating the Beauty They Bring to Your Daily Life

We know that plants help rid the air of toxins and generate oxygen. This is a fact that has been scientifically proven. Although according to NASA, to really achieve this in our homes we would need about one thousand plants per 100 square feet (9.2 sq. m). Sometimes I feel up to that challenge, but I think I'd be met with opposition from the people I live with. Haters. But to cleanse the air and produce oxygen, couldn't plants just be a stick with simple, green leaves? They would still photosynthesize and perform all the functions of producing oxygen in a much simpler form, each one like the other, absent of anything interesting. But they are not sticks with simple, green leaves. Instead, plants come in every magnificent shape, color, texture, and leaf pattern imaginable!

Plants could just as easily cleanse the air and make oxygen if they were in the form of plain old sticks and green leaves. But they are not! They are magnificent things of beauty, like my *Philodendron* 'Pink Princess' whom I call Grace Jones for obvious reasons—she is fierce! It's not just oxygen plants provide, it's also beauty (something there is never too much of).

I have plants that are naturally pink and black. Pink and black! I never imagined such a thing existed before I started collecting plants. I have others that look as if Georgia O'Keeffe hand-painted each individual leaf. The way they look boggles my brain. I find their varied appearance to be a thing of wonder. I often ask myself, "What does it all mean?" Do these beauties hold some sort of hidden code in the patterns on their leaves? The more I try to find the answer, the more questions I have: Are aliens real? Is Tupac alive? Why did Kylo Ren kiss Rey? Will we ever get that Arya Stark spinoff? Was Snape really good, or was that just a last-minute plot twist? Oops, I digress. Back to the question at hand: Why do plants look the way they look? To that question I think only one answer exists from the human perspective, and it is a simple one. They look the way they look just for the sake of beauty. They simply give us a double dose of gratuitous beauty. When we look at objectively beautiful things, I think it boosts our serotonin and produces endorphins. It just makes us feel good. If there is one thing we have learned over these past few years, we all need more simple beauty in our daily lives.

Plants are an easy way to make the space we live in our sanctuary. The space where we come to relax and recharge can, and should, be your home. It's the place you probably spend the most of your time, so fill it with beauty. Do you have that one room where everyone just drops stuff? The room that has amassed all the stuff that you really should toss but haven't gotten around to sorting? I had one of those rooms. It was full of beach shoes and bags, last winter's hats and boots, and a few plastic tubs of my kids'

old clothes that I couldn't toss because I was too sentimentally attached to them. It was just a total dumping ground for things we could not find a place for. But you know what else it had? Great light! And it was being wasted on a space that no one wanted to enter.

One afternoon, I opened the door to add one more bag of clutter to the mess and the golden light filled the room with such a magical glow it stopped me in my tracks. I stepped over the bags blocking the doorway and stood in the middle of the room. Right there in that moment, I decided to clear out all that useless junk and reclaim that room. After sorting and tossing many things—I held onto those cute little suede moccasins, though, and those handknit sweaters—the room was finally clear. I could not believe we were wasting that space. I gave it a fresh coat of paint (pink of course, because I didn't have nearly enough of that color in my life) and added some wallpaper. Standing in the middle of the room flooded with light, I couldn't believe that I hadn't thought of doing what came next sooner. I filled it with plants. What was once a wasteland became my own tropical oasis! And the light is perfect for growing everything from hoyas to pothos.

While having a room dedicated to plants is very nice, it's also wonderful having plants in all of the rooms. Plants will liven any décor in any room. I love plants, as you well know. But my first love is books. I have combined the two and drape all of my bookshelves with plants. When I look at my shelves, I can't even remember how they looked without the plants. Just books? How boring. Plants brighten the space and really help you fall in love with your home. A fully furnished room, no matter the décor, is empty without plants.

This *Ficus elastica* 'Tineke', commonly known as the variegated rubber plant, looks like a paint-by-numbers masterpiece.

This room was once a wasteland of forgotten seasonal junk. I could not let that good light go unused. It is now one of my favorite rooms in the house. When decorating with plants, don't stop at potted plants. This wallpaper brings all the drama with its tropical leaf motif. I love it so much, I've used it in two other rooms in my house since hanging it here.

Plan a plant takeover

Not ready to pop up a grow tent in your living room? Here are a few tips for incorporating plants into any style of décor:

- **Add floating shelves.** You can create living art for your walls with a floating plant shelf. Install a grouping of shelves with staggered heights or a single shelf for drama. Stage the shelf using a mix of upright and trailing plants or add framed photos and decorative art objects.

- **Use plants on bookshelves.** Plants look great on a bookshelf, either mixed in with books or on their own. A plant trailing down from the top is pure beauty! If the back of the shelf is closed, don't forget to rotate your plants to keep their growth even.

- **Fill empty corners.** Add a hanging grow light and dress them up with a statuesque floor plant! I have never met a monstera or bird of paradise plant that wasn't ready for the spotlight!

- **Utilize the empty space behind the sofa.** Add a console table and, of course, plants. Add two decorative table lamps, swap out the bulbs for full-spectrum light bulbs, and you can choose any plant you want for that space.

- **Forget fabric, hang a plant curtain at the window instead.** Use a clothing rod, rather than a curtain rod. It comes further out from the wall than a curtain rod, making more room to hang plants of different sizes. Add S hooks and hanging plant holders. Opt for macrame hangers for a boho vibe or minimal leather hangers for a clean, modern look.

- **Decorate with foliage, not flowers.** Use potted plants for your table center-piece instead. They last longer, and if it's color you want, there are plenty of colorful variegated plants.

This round shelf used to house books, photos, knickknacks, and just a few plants. Slowly I kept adding more plants and taking away books, until it was a total plant takeover. It serves as a beautiful living focal point in the room. It never stays the same for too long. The styling possibilities are endless, and plants are frequently swapped for fresh new looks.

What Is Your Light Like?

When you bring any plants into your home, this is the first question you should ask yourself, "What is my light like?" Not all light is created equal. Knowing this is a surefire way to get on the path to successful growing. The easiest way to find out that answer is to learn which direction your windows are facing. Whip out the compass app on your phone and get to mapping those windows. Once you know what lighting conditions you have, you can figure out which plants will thrive in your environment and what the watering needs will be. The formula is generally the brighter the light, the more frequently a plant will need watering (except for desert types of cacti and succulents, of course).

YOU KNOW WHICH WAY IS UP. NOW WHAT?

- **North-facing.** This is indirect light. Take a look out the window up at the sky, if all you see is blue but not the sun, this is indirect light. It is the least intense of the lighting conditions, some might even call it low. However, there are many green beauties that thrive in this light.

- **South-facing.** This is direct, bright light. It is the brightest of bright light. This is the plant parent's dream—to have a ton of south-facing windows. Sun-worshipping plants will get hours of direct sun here. Not a sun worshipper? Simply move the plant back from the window or add curtains or blinds to filter the bright light.

- **East-facing.** This is a mix of medium to low light. You'll get a couple of hours of direct, bright light in the early part of the day, then indirect, bright light in the afternoon.

- **West-facing.** This is medium light. It is a mix of indirect, bright light in the morning and bright, direct light later in the day. This is great for plants that love the sun, but not too much.

Not all light is created equal. Knowing the direction your windows face will help you figure out whether you have direct, bright light, or indirect light. The different types of light have different levels of intensity and are suited for different types of plants. This south-facing window serves up hours of very bright, direct light. My very small collection of succulents and a few cacti love this location.

One of the ways you can tell that your plant is not getting adequate light is that it will get "leggy" as it tries to stretch and grow toward the light. I placed this *Begonia maculata* on a back shelf and kind of forgot about it. It went completely lopsided and fell over. No amount of rotating at that point was going to help. I gave it a trellis for support and a bright new location. With the trellis and new home, it is now getting a more even distribution of light on the entire plant.

Top Plant Picks for North-Facing Light

COMMON NAME	BOTANICAL NAME	HUMIDITY LEVEL	MOISTURE LEVEL
Burle Marx philodendron	*Philodendron burle-marxii*	Adapts to average household humidity	Dry between watering
Calathea or rattlesnake plant	*Goeppertia insignis (Calathea lancifolia)*	Humidity lover	Likes to be evenly moist, cannot withstand drought
Emerald Beauty aglaonema	*Aglaonema commutatum* 'Emerald Beauty'	Adapts to average household humidity	Can tolerate some drought
Fingers anthurium	*Anthurium pedatoradiatum*	Adapts to average household humidity	Likes to remain evenly moist, not soggy
Memoria Corsii dumb cane or dieffenbachia	*Dieffenbachia* 'Memoria Corsii'	Can adapt to average household humidity but will thrive in higher humidity	Likes to be evenly moist, cannot withstand drought; will droop very dramatically with a missed watering
Regal Shields alocasia	*Alocasia* 'Regal Shields'	Can adapt to average household humidity but will thrive in higher humidity	Likes to dry between watering
Swiss cheese plant	*Monstera deliciosa*	Adapts to average household humidity	Can tolerate some drought
Triostar Stromanthe	*Stromanthe sanguinea* 'Triostar'	Can adapt to average household humidity but will thrive in higher humidity	Likes to be evenly moist but can withstand a missed watering

The *Stromanthe sanguinea* 'Triostar', with its beautiful painterly leaves, does well in north-facing light. Too much light and this beauty will lose some of the gorgeous color that caught your eye in the first place.

Top Plant Picks for South-Facing Light

COMMON NAME	BOTANICAL NAME	HUMIDITY LEVEL	MOISTURE LEVEL
Burro's tail	*Sedum morganianum*	Easily adapts to household humidity	Let dry completely between waterings
Birkin or White Wave philodendron	*Philodendron* 'Birkin' or 'White Wave'	Easily adapts to household humidity	Likes to be evenly moist; allow to dry between waterings
Bunny ear cactus	*Opuntia microdasys*	Easily adapts to household humidity	Let dry completely between waterings
Exotica wax vine	*Hoya carnosa* 'Exotica'	Can adapt to average household humidity but will thrive in increased humidity	Let dry between watering; period of drought encourages blooms
Jade plant	*Crassula ovata*	Easily adapts to household humidity	Let dry completely between waterings
Rubber plant	*Ficus elastica*	Can adapt to average household humidity but will thrive in increased humidity	Can tolerate some drought but thrives when watered regularly
Splash wax vine	*Hoya pubicalyx* 'Splash'	Can adapt to average but will thrive in increased humidity	Let dry between watering; period of drought encourages blooms
String of pearls	*Curio (Senecio) rowleyanus*	Easily adapts to household humidity	Let dry completely between waterings

To say that I am obsessed with this plant is an understatement. This succulent is a *Curio (Senecio) rowleyanus*, more commonly known as a string of pearls. This beauty hangs in a south-facing window and gets hours of direct light. I wish I could tell you that this plant ended up on my head for the first time only for this photo, but that would be a lie. When I take it down to water it, I may or may not dance around with it on my head first. I will neither admit nor deny this tidbit.

When windows are not enough

Even knowing the direction of your windows, you still may not have enough natural light. I have sixteen windows on the front of my house. That sounds like a lot, right? It sounds like my house should be flooded with incredible natural light. But it isn't. The front of the house is facing north, and half of the windows are heavily shaded by a covered porch. That is where grow lights come in handy. Grow lights are every indoor gardener's friend. I have them in all of the rooms on the first floor. My plants would not survive without this supplemental light. Thankfully, grow lights come in every style imaginable because I need them to blend in. You can find them in floor lamps with bendable necks, in sleek hanging lights, and even in track lights. Many of the styles blend into any décor. And you don't have to stop there. I have replaced all the ordinary bulbs in my table lamps in the living room with full-spectrum bulbs that act as grow lights. The full-spectrum bulbs and the grow light bulbs are all LED so they are energy efficient and will not put a strain on your monthly utility bill. No matter the weather outside, it's sunny inside my house thanks to my grow lights. This is an added benefit during the gray days of winter.

With the help of hanging grow lights, I am finally able to have a fiddle-leaf fig in a windowless corner. Don't let lack of light stop you from adding plants to your home—just add a grow light.

CHAPTER 7

There Is No One-Size-Fits-All

A Twisty Journey to a Green Thumb—
Sometimes Plants Die. Try Again.

There is no such thing as a green thumb. There is only patience, perseverance, a willingness to learn, and acceptance of the fact that you will kill a few plants. It is par for the course and part of the learning process. Get used to that real quick. Often times, we put this extraordinary pressure on ourselves to be absolutely amazing at everything from our very first try. Where is the fun in that? Where is the room for growth? (See what I did right there?) You don't have to be good at something as soon as you try it. In fact, you may never be "good at it." The key is to focus on the process, not the outcome. Learning something new, in and of itself, is an accomplishment. You can be absolutely horrible at it, and you can fail miserably in your initial attempts. The important thing is to keep trying. Keep growing (oops, I did it again!).

Along this plant journey I have killed so very many plants. Some over and over, like my *Calathea orbifolia*. It was the very first calathea that I discovered, and I fell madly and deeply in love with it. Each time I bought that plant, I killed it. And with each failure, I sort of learned what not to do the next time. I always knew there would be a next time, even when I publicly declared there would not be a next time. Now when I say "no more calatheas" anyone who hears me say it knows not to believe me. There will certainly be a next time. They are just too beautiful to resist. I could never just walk past it—well I did walk past one that one time and, to this day, I still regret it. The plant was HUGE, the biggest I'd ever seen in real life. But I was just fresh off the heartbreak of having had one die on me, and I wasn't ready to revisit that pain. But then I did. And I finally found some success after learning from my past failures. It remains to be seen whether I learned all of the things for success. But the point is, I'm not afraid to try. Failure is okay. Failure is a key component to succeeding because it teaches you what does not work. Your plant journey will be filled with successes and failures—each will teach you. Receive the lessons.

It's Okay for Things to Be Out of Your Control

There is an even greater lesson that I learned from my plants. Plants will teach us the art of letting go of the need to control things. As an admitted control freak, this has been the greatest lesson of all. As plant parents, we can do all the things—careful watering, fertilizing, giving good light—and the plant may still not grow as fast or as full as we want it to. It may even die. This can happen for any number of reasons, all of them beyond our control. What you learn is, you can only be responsible for your effort, but you are not in control of the outcome. This truly applies across all aspects of life—our relationship with our partners, our spouses, our children, our co-workers. Do your level best. Do all of the things that you are able to do. But let go of the emotional investment in wanting to control how things will turn out. Almost 90 percent of the time you are not in control of the outcome, even when you think you are. Control is really just an illusion. We have no way of knowing or controlling how things will end up, no matter our best efforts.

PLANT CARE IS NONLINEAR

Plant care is nonlinear because we all have different environments. When it comes to growing plants indoors, there are so many variables involved there couldn't possibly be one way of doing things. All those absolute rules are rubbish. There are no absolutes beyond the fact that you absolutely cannot grow a plant in a dark, windowless bathroom. That is a fact that cannot be disputed. I used to think the absolute was drainage holes, but I have seen people successfully grow plants in pots without a hole. I wouldn't dare try, but I have seen some do it. I am just too heavy-handed with my watering for that to ever work.

Knowing who you are as a plant parent is also why plant care is nonlinear. We all have different Shaolin kung fu styles. And no matter what advice I dole out, some of it will make sense for your growing environment and lifestyle, and some may not. Take what works, toss the rest. Ultimately, you must find what works for you. Whatever one way I'm growing a particular plant, I assure you there is another way to grow that very same plant in a totally different environment. Even after you've asked all the questions, read all the books, gone down the rabbit hole online, the plant may still die. And it's quite possible it has nothing to do with you (or you overwatered it). Sometimes they just die. Dump the plant, wash and save the pot. Get a new plant, try again.

Here friend, take this. This little cutie is the *Pilea peperomioides*, also known as the "pass it on plant." It literally propagates itself by growing little pups like the one I'm holding. Someone gave me one when I first started collecting plants, and I have since shared pups with so many who did not have a single plant. From that one little plant their collection grew as they fell in love with the act of caring for plants. Anyone can grow houseplants. You do not need any prior experience or skill. You can also be really bad at it at first. All you need to grow houseplants is a willingness to learn and to keep trying.

MANAGE YOUR EXPECTATIONS

I think this is the most important piece of advice that I can give anyone about anything ever—manage your expectations. How much easier would life be if we managed our expectations in all things? Whether it's a new relationship, how your kids will turn out, that dress you just ordered online, or the new plant you just bought. We want it all to turn out spectacularly, to be everything we have always dreamed of. Don't stop doing that. Just leave some room for when things don't turn out exactly as you had hoped. And just because it's not exactly as you hoped doesn't mean it all went to hell. Why is it all or nothing? Add a dash of pragmatism to those high hopes. And this is coming from a Pisces. Our entire existence seems to be up in the clouds, in some watery dreamscape. Pisces don't come crashing down when things are less than we hoped for because even though our head is in the clouds, we are going with the flow. We keep right on swimming if the stream changes from the direction we hoped it would go. We know there is always that possibility.

This is how you should approach plant parenthood. Plants in nature are not perfect. Yet somehow, when we bring them into our homes, we suddenly expect perfect from them. Leaves will yellow, edges will crisp, and blooms fade. This is all the normal life cycle of a plant, no matter your growing experience. If we are expecting perfection from these living green beings, we will be sorely disappointed. The other truth is, sometimes plants die. And it will have little to do with you. Some plants are in it for the very long haul and can be passed on from generation to generation.

Yes! You read that right! My neighbor across the street shared a cutting with me from a hoya that has been in her family for over fifty years. Fifty years! It was passed down to her from her aunt, who received it from her mother. It is the most magnificent *Hoya carnosa* that I have ever laid eyes upon outside of a botanical garden. During the warm summer months, she hangs it in her front yard for all to witness its glory. It literally explodes with blooms. There are as many clusters of delicate pink flowers as there are leaves. It is truly a sight to behold.

My mother, two of my aunts, and my sister all have a *Dieffenbachia* 'Tropic Snow' in their homes. Their plants all came from a single plant that has been propagated and shared around our family for the past twenty years or so. The mother plant was affectionally nicknamed Dorothy, and that name has stuck for all of the different households. But not all plants are like that fifty-year-old hoya or Dorothy. Some are here just for a spell, a limited time of enjoyment. And the sooner you accept that, the happier you will be when you bring them home.

I love calatheas. I have tried ending our relationship many times, but we have a hold on each other. Yes, I'm saying it's a two-way street because they seem to be everywhere I am. Coincidence? I don't think so. I've come to accept the fact that they will not likely survive the winter here in my dry home. I mean, I'm going to try and help them survive to the very best of my ability. But I'm no longer deeply invested in their survival, and don't take it as a personal affront when they give up the ghost. Now I think of them like they are cut flowers, and I just enjoy them while they last.

I used to swear off of *Calathea orbifolia* after I'd kill one, and then I would backslide and buy another. I have since stopped swearing off of them—I can't quit them because I love them so. Instead, I have come to manage my expectations. They do great during the summer when I can bring them outside to soak up the warm, humid air. When the season changes and I have to bring them back inside, I do not expect them to look the way they looked during the summer. I just cross my fingers, hope for the best, and enjoy it while it lasts.

HAPPY PLANTS, HAPPY YOU

While this has been a solo adventure, my family has also reaped the benefits. Adding plants to our home has added a literal breath of fresh air and made the rooms come alive! Plants make this room inviting and cozy. The light bulbs in the table lamps have been replaced with full-spectrum bulbs. No matter the weather outside, its sunny in here! A fully furnished room is empty without plants.

CHAPTER 8

Plant Care Is Self-Care (And It's Badass!)

Check In on Yourself by Checking In on Your Plants

As my collection grew and I was spending more time with my plants, I quickly learned they were much more than a hobby or design tool. When I carved out time to care for plants, I was intentionally carving out time to care for myself. Growing plants indoors was something that I did entirely for me and the joy it made me feel. It was something that I did to quiet the chatter in my head, to slow down, and to find leisure. The more I committed to these acts, the more committed I became to carving out time for caring for myself. And it had to be real quality time that was spent alone with my thoughts and emotions. It was not something that I was used to doing. Before plants, my idea of self-care or taking time for myself was pretty one-note. For the most part, it was something I neglected to do, but when I did, the time spent was task based—like getting my nails or hair done. Now that's not to say that those things aren't great, but it wasn't really time spent with myself.

You cannot fully relax and recharge if you are wrestling with guilt. Plants helped me recognize how useless that emotion is. Being surrounded by plants gives me such a sense of joy and relief. When I said yes to plants, I said yes to me.

Plants provided a means for carving out meaningful leisure time alone. I was not watching a clock or paying for a service in a crowded salon with a cacophony of noises and fumes. Plants were a real path to peace. I was conditioned to feel guilty whenever I put my needs ahead of others, or when I took time out for myself to do nothing at all. Before plants, I always felt the pull of familial obligation, and, instead of making off for some alone time, I would include everyone. I think sometimes they accepted the invitations out of that same sense of obligation.

I love tiny things, as much as I love plants. I have a collection of weird, tiny animal figurines that I've gathered over the years. Obviously, they don't take up much space, so no one really notices the tiny little animal menagerie on my dresser. Sure, we all loved museums, but did my friends and family really want to spend hours traveling to see that exhibit of miniatures? When I look back on it, I think the answer is a resounding no. I think sometimes my family felt a sense of obligation to go along because I'd planned the outing, and I felt obligated to drag them along, thinking they'd be bored at home. While everyone had a perfectly fine time, they would have been quite content to send me off on my own to ooohh and ahhh over the world's largest collecting of minis at that museum without worrying whether they were having a good time or were bored to tears.

When I began my plant journey, I kept it all for me. This newfound thing brought me so much joy I wanted to guard and protect it. I did not want anyone's lack of interest or disinclination to dampen my interest and enthusiasm. So this time, I was perfectly content to make this thing all my own. And while I may not have invited them along on this plant journey, my happy was infectious. My family felt thrilled for me, without having to reluctantly join in. And for the first time in I don't know how long, I did not feel at all guilty

for doing something entirely for myself. As it turns out, making time for myself did not mean I had less time for others. Where I felt restricted before, like there was never enough hours in the day, it suddenly felt like time had expanded and there was enough. I didn't actually get an extra hour in the day, but I did gain something in what I left behind. I left behind useless guilt and the unreasonable sense of obligation and duty to everything. By taking time for myself in a manner that was both leisurely and filled with abundant beauty, I relieved myself of stress and worry. Being good to myself truly did make it so much easier to be good to others. Doing things out of guilt and a false sense of obligation will not get anyone's needs met. We tend to feel guilt when putting ourselves first, when in fact it is not a selfish act. How can you be good to others if you are not good to yourself? Plants are my pleasure principle. I have them purely for the sake of beauty and enjoyment and happiness. It's fantastic!

Plants are my guilt-free pleasure. While no one in my house joined in on fawning over a new leaf, they also reaped the benefits of having nature indoors. The once dark and empty corners are now filled with lush, tropical plants. And because they are windowless corners, that means I must use a grow light. That artificial sunlight is nothing short of a wonder during the grey days of winter. No matter what the weather is outdoors, it's always bright and cheery and green inside our home. Plants trailing from the ceiling and bookshelves literally give the rooms new life. When I relax and recharge with plants, I do not feel any sense of guilt. The benefits they bring go beyond just me personally. While I am not sharing this journey directly with them, my family is on it with me. Plants have changed our lives in so many good ways even without them picking up a watering can. Although I would like some help with the repotting.

Widening the Circle

While I enjoyed taking care of my indoor plants at home, I began to feel a need to widen my circle. Caring for these plants and watching them thrive under my care was delightful! These are tropical plants that I was able to keep alive in a decidedly nontropical environment. And not just alive, they are thriving. My fiddle-leaf fig that started as a thirty-six inch (91 cm) plant in a gallon-sized (3.8 L) pot is now over seven feet (2.1 m) tall! It would be taller, but I've had to trim it when it reached the ceiling. I have plants in every room and can rattle off their names and care needs on demand. Some are commercially rare and hard to find, others you'd see at every garden store—but all of them are precious to me.

My collection was dreamy! But I really wanted to talk about my plants with other people who understood the excitement of a new leaf or spotting what looked like a peduncle on one of my hoyas. My nonplant friends and family nodded and listened politely, but I could see their eyes glaze over when I went on too long about my plants. I was not fooled by their feigned interest. I needed more. I wanted to trade stories of plant successes and failures. The failures were sometimes really funny! Nonplant collecting friends just did not understand why buying another *Begonia rex* was both uproariously funny and tragic. I wanted to find a few like-minded people with whom I could unabashedly geek out over a plant with new growth. I wanted someone to match my enthusiasm when I finally found my wish list plant at a local nursery. Since there was no Tinder for people looking for plant-friends (I wanted someone to send me nodes, not nudes) I started an Instagram account for my plants, and PlantBlerd was born. To my very happy surprise, instead of finding a few like-minded people, I found an entire community of like-minded people who totally matched my enthusiasm and outsized interest in plants.

COMMUNITY CARE IS SELF-CARE

When we talk about self-care we think about, well, "self." It's right there in the word. But I think a big part of self-care is also community care. Finding people with shared interests and passions is affirming. Finding community gives you a sense of belonging and affirms that the weird stuff you are into is not just weird, it's also super cool. Of course, you don't need community to care for yourself, but people need people. The path to peace is so much sweeter when it is not walked alone. I thought I would find a few people who liked plants. Instead, what I found were many people who not only liked plants but were generous with their welcoming, support, and encouragement.

For you to understand how huge this was for me, I have to take you back a little in time. I grew up in a very small town in Connecticut. We moved there when I was in the third grade. It was small. Like really, really small—we had a volunteer fire department, no streetlights, and random fields with cows. Not farms, just fields with cows. I felt like a fish out of water in that town. And not just because I'm a Pisces, but because no one matched my vibe or my energy. To the people in that very small town, my interests were not weird and cool—they were just weird. I left that town on the first thing smoking as soon as I had the chance. And while I have been long gone from that small town, and have plenty of friends, I still sometimes had that fish out of water feeling when it came to shared interests. In fellow plant people, I have found my community. When there is a plant event, I can just roll up alone and feel right at home. You will hear it said that plant people are some of the very best people. I can confirm that to be very true. We are all rooting for each other.

Plant Care is Self-Care
and Self-Care is Badass!

Putting yourself on the to-do list is not a selfish act. It is an act of self-perseveration, and that is rule number one. If you use yourself up in the service of everyone and everything else, there will be nothing left. There will be no reservoir to draw from when you need it, because you have given it all away. Don't give it all away to your job, your friends, and your family. You have to save something for yourself. We've been conditioned to think we have to hustle nonstop and work like maniacs. We feel that the minute we take time for ourselves, someone hungrier or more ambitious will be waiting in the wings to claim the spot. It's simply not true. The only thing true is that never stopping to care for yourself is going to lead to burnout, resentment, and feelings of being unfulfilled. It's okay to take time for yourself. We know this, but sometimes we need to hear it again. Sometimes we need to be reminded of the real truth—your relationship with yourself deserves the same nurturing, care, and attention that you give to others.

When you bring plants into your home, your new-found botanical besties can help you pave a guilt-free path to peace and self-care. And when you start actually caring for yourself in a meaningful way, a whole world opens up. Time expands rather than constricts. The world on your shoulders gets lighter. Self-care does not require fanfare and hoopla. It just needs you, your intention, and a plant. You cannot be good to others if you are not good to yourself. Plant care is self-care and self-care is badass! So, buy yourself a new plant today, and let it put you on a path to peace.

This planter is the focal point of any room. It was gifted to me by my mom. And when I say gifted, I mean I convinced her to give it to me after I spotted it on her deck. As the OG Plant Parent, her house is still the best place to "shop" for plant accessories!

Shopping for plants is fun. It's even better when you do it with plant friends! But be warned, you will blow your budget. Pictured from left to right: Taji Riley @unboundbx_, Dominique Edouard @domslittlegarden, Niyya Tenee @thebloomjourney, Kevin Edouard @theplantpapi

Resources

MY FAVORITE ONLINE PLANT STORES
for when I can't make it to the store or when
I'm looking for that one particular plant:

Plant Proper | plantproper.com
Grounded | feelgrounded.com
Steve's Leaves | stevesleaves.com
Tennessee Tropicals | tennesseetropicals.com
The Leafy Branch | theleafybranch.com
Plant the Jungle | plantthejungle.com
Centered by Plants (Canada) | centeredbyplants.ca
Prick (UK) | prickldn.com

I can take some of the credit, but not all, for keeping my plants
alive. Here are the tools and products I can't do without:

GROW LIGHTS
Soltech | soltech.com
Rousseau Plant Care | rousseauplant.care
Sansi | sansiled.com

FERTILIZER
Liqui-Dirt Organics | liquidirt.com
Big Bloom Liquid Plant Food | FoxFarm | foxfarm.com

SOIL AND SOIL AMENDMENTS
Ocean Forest Potting Soil | FoxFarm | foxfarm.com
Big & Chunky Perlite | FoxFarm | foxfarm.com
Cactus Mix | Espoma Company | espoma.com
Orchid Mix | Espoma Company | espoma.com

PEST CONTROL
When neem is not enough:
Mite-X | BONIDE | bonide.com
Systemic Houseplant Insect Control | BONIDE | bonide.com
Captain Jack's DeadBug Brew | BONIDE | bonide.com

WATERING
Watering spikes | Blumat | blumat.com

About the Author

Kamili Bell Hill combined her love of plants and design and curated a brand and community known as PlantBlerd. She noticed there were not many social pages that highlighted houseplant collectors who looked like her, and so she also founded BlackPeople.wPlants. She is a voracious reader, lover of the arts, and a certified Potter Head (as in Harry Potter). She put a career in law on hold to pursue her true passion of interior design and quickly realized the important role plants play in her designs for clients.

Kamili combines beautiful houseplants with simple care information and words of encouragement, using engaging language and humor that is widely relatable. PlantBlerd serves as both a style and a growing guide.

BlackPeople.wPlants features Black houseplant collectors from around the world. Her followers are loyal and highly engaged.

Find more from Kamili on TikTok and Instagram:
@plantblerd
@blackpeople.wplants

Acknowledgments

I can't believe I wrote a book! If you are reading this, that means not only did I write a book, but it was published and purchased. It still doesn't seem real to me, but it is indeed very real! There are some people whom I have to thank, for without them you'd still be reading, but you would not be reading *this* book.

First, I must thank my beautiful little family. To my incredible husband Eddie, thank you for being my person. Thank you for being the architect of this beautiful life we have built together. You are the very best cheerleader a person could wish for. On the days when the whispers of self-doubt were at their loudest, you silenced them. Your constant support and encouragement were the good luck charms that I needed. Thank you for reading and re-reading every single draft—even when the change was just a word or two. Your patience and objective feedback were priceless. On a sunny day in September many years ago, I said that I was lucky and blessed to have you. Those words are as true today as they were then.

To my incredible daughters Skye and Lyric, thank you for helping me grow each and every day. I look at you two, and I know that the future is bright because you are both in it. I now see the world through your eyes, and it is full of wonder.

You are both so much cooler than I ever was, and I am just so proud to be your mother. What an honor it is to help guide you along life's path. You are indeed my very best propagations.

Thank you to my mother Beverly, the *original* plant parent. You filled our home with love and green. Long before plants were trending on social media, you had pothos vines draped on the windows, and ficus trees tucked in every corner (I still say you need to move that fiddle-leaf fig). And let's not forget the ferns—I still don't know how you do it. You made me appreciate the value and importance of making the space you call home beautiful and peaceful. No matter the size or location, it can have beauty in it. When I look around my own home, I see your influences everywhere. Thank you for being the standard by which all things are measured.

Thank you to my framily—my siblings—Rashaad, Jihan, Cami, and Kenny, my many aunts, uncles, cousins, and nieces and nephews. Life is a party with you in it. But, of course, family is not just the family you're born to or marry into, it's also the family you *choose*. Thank you to everyone who makes up the fabric of my life—from my beloved BBBs book club sisters to my plant-enabling friends, and everyone in between. You make my life lush and full like a newly purchased calathea!

Tribe Vibe! Self-care does not mean going it alone. Community care is an important part of any self-care journey. There is nothing better than finding like-minded people to share in the journey of care. Pictured top row: Tia Curtis @thequeer_bungalow, Colah B. Tawkin @blackinthegarden, Niyya Tenee @thebloomjourney. Pictured middle row: myself, Veronica Moore @brownskinplantmama, Brayan Pinto @brotherearthh. Pictured bottom row: Hunter, Veronica Moore's daughter

And just like that *Calathea orbifolia*, I'll never give you up! There is no self-care without community care because people need people. Thank you for always lifting me up and supporting me through the highs and the lows, the twists and turns, and the fungus gnat infestations. Thank you for your generosity of spirit and time. And most of all, thank you for rooting for me! (You see what I did right there?)

Thank you to the entire team at The Quarto Group and Cool Springs Press. Thank you for making the process for this first-time author absolutely painless. Thank you for your guidance and confidence in me. And an extra special thank you to Jessica Walliser for seeing me. This has been one of the happiest surprises of my life. Before there were plants there were books. To now have a published book of my own is beyond a dream come true.

There are words, and then there are the pictures. Thank you to Christina Bohn for listening to my ramblings and capturing such beautiful images that fully bring the words in this book to life.

Thank you, Paula Champagne, for adding yet another layer of beauty to this book! I remember when I bought prints of your amazing work for my daughters' rooms, and now we are working together. Life is nothing short of amazing. It has been an honor!

Last but not leaf (I'm sorry I just couldn't resist it), thank you to my plant family—online, and in real life. Thank you for coming along on this incredibly unexpected journey. Never in my wildest dreams did I think that that first post on my PlantBlerd account (it was a Crispy Wave fern on my nightstand) would grow into *this*! Thank you for allowing me to Blerd out over plants with wanton abandon. You have helped that little girl who felt like a fish out of water for much of her life find her place in this world. Thank you for sharing the joy of a new leaf, and the thrill of that long-awaited hoya bloom, and for the encouragement to try again when a plant dies (why is it always a calathea?). Sometimes the path is winding, just go with it. It'll lead you to where you are supposed to be. It led me here, and I am eternally grateful.

"Today is where your book begins. The rest is still unwritten." *Unwritten*, Natasha Bedingfield.

Index

Bolded page numbers refer to photographs.

A
aeration
  benefits, 68–69
  fiddle-leaf fig, 28
  fingers anthurium, **69**
  soil amendments for, 118
  soil refreshment and, 120
  tools for, 28, 68, **69**
ambulatory meditation, 120,
  122–123

B
bacteria
  horticultural charcoal and, 118
  Mycobacterium vaccae, 108
  soil and, 108
  water propagation and, 54
blooms
  drought and, 103, 147
  H. callistophylla, 103
  Hoya bilobata, **102**
  Hoya carnosa, **44**, 45, 147, 154
  Hoya macrophylla, 103
  Hoya pubicalyx, 147
  inflorescences as, 34, **34**
  reward of, 89

C
cacti
  light for, **140**, 141, 147
  terra cotta pots for, 116
  watering, 141
calatheas
  deaths of, 152, 154, **155**
  horticultural charcoal for, 118
  indirect light and, 143
  mealybugs and, 125
  pots for, 116
  spider mites and, 75, 128
castile soap
  leaf shine with, 78, **78**, 80

as pesticide, 74, 80
Ceylon cinnamon
  as pesticide, 71
  propagation with, 59
community, 112, 163

D
deaths
  acceptance of, 91–92, 151–152
  control and, 153
  environment and, 94, 96
  expectation management, 154
  learning from, 151, 152, 153
  nonlinear plant care and, 153
décor
  bookshelves and, 134, 138
  Boston ferns as, **90–91**
  decorative pots, 116, 120,
    164–165
  dedicated plant rooms, 134,
    136–137
  empty corners, 138
  entrances, **11**
  fiddle-leaf fig as, 23
  floating shelves, 138
  focal points, **164–165**
  full-spectrum lightbulbs,
    156–157
  groupings, **138–139**
  grow lights, 148
  plant curtains, 138
  pothos as, **39**
  round shelves, **138–139**
  snake plants as, **42–43**
  variety and, 38
  wallpaper, **136–137**
drainage. *See also* water
  aeration and, 68
  ceramic pots, 116
  decorative pots, 120
  drainage holes, 68, 70, 82, 101,
    114–115, 116, 120, 153
  horticultural charcoal and, 118
  hydrophobic soil and, 101

orchid bark and, 118, **118**
  pebbly trays and, 82
  plastic pots, 116
  soil and, 118, **118**
  window screen and, **114–115**
drought. *See also* water
  Aglaonema, 47, 143
  calathea, 143
  exotica wax vine, 147
  fungus gnats, 71
  hoya blooms, 103
  Memoria Corsii, 143
  rattlesnake plant, 143
  rubber plant, 147
  snake plant, 42
  splash wax vine, 147
  succulents, 116, **117**
  Swiss cheese plant, 143
  terra cotta pots, 116, **117**
  ZZ plant, 41

E
epiphytes, **33**, 112, 118
equipment. *See* supplies

F
ferns
  asparagus fern, **88**
  Boston fern, 17, 36, **90–91**,
    91–92
  Crispy Wave fern, 94, **95**, 96
  environment and, 92, 94
  horticultural charcoal for, 118
  maidenhair fern, 92, **92–93**, 94
  mealybugs and, 74
  pots for, 116
fertilizers
  application amounts, 29
  application frequency, 29
  fiddle-leaf fig, 25, 28
  granular fertilizers, 29
  hoya blooms and, 103
  liquid fertilizer, 29, 59, 79, 103
  NPK fertilizer, 28, 29